THE CONFIDENCE SWITCH

FLIPPING THE FEAR OF BEING SEEN

ALEC JOHNSON

Published by Digital Stage Publishing

www.takeonetech.io

ISBN: 978-1-0676112-0-0 (Paperback)

ISBN: 978-1-0676112-1-7 (Hardback)

First edition, 2026

The stories in this book are based on real experiences. Some names and identifying details have been changed to protect the privacy of individuals.

This book is intended for general informational purposes only and does not constitute professional advice. The author and publisher accept no responsibility for any outcomes arising from the application of the ideas presented in this book.

For May, Jasmine, Emily and Dale.
You're the reason showing up matters.

CONTENTS

PREFACE

This book wasn't supposed to happen. Not this soon, anyway. It began as a short video course, a seven-day challenge to help people get more confident on camera. Something simple, actionable and bite-sized.

But the more I created, the more I realised: this was about far more than video. It was about the stories we tell ourselves, the pressure to perform, the fear of being seen and the myth that confidence is something reserved for other people.

I knew I couldn't stop at a short course because I've lived this journey firsthand. I've stood on stages speaking to thousands and felt completely at ease, then later found myself freezing up the moment I looked into a lens. I've spent weeks recording ten-minute videos because I couldn't get the "perfect take," letting perfectionism, fear and self-doubt steal time, momentum and joy from something that was meant to feel meaningful.

But I've also come out the other side. Not by mastering performance, but by letting go of it. By switching my focus from trying to look confident to simply showing up as myself.

That's what this book is about. It's not a manual for getting better on camera. It's a framework for remembering the version of you that already knows how to speak, connect and lead.

I wrote this for anyone who's held back their message because they didn't feel "ready," for anyone who's let the fear of judgment drown out the pull of purpose and for anyone who's felt like confidence was something they needed to earn.

It isn't.

You don't need to become someone else. You just need to become who you already are.

This is your switch.

Let's flip it.

Alec

ACKNOWLEDGMENTS

First, I want to thank you, the reader. Without your desire to show up, learn and grow, this book wouldn't have its purpose. Every time you choose to challenge yourself, to face your fears and to step into your value, you make the world a better place.

To my family, thank you for your patience, support and understanding as I've worked through my own relationship with confidence. Your belief in me keeps me grounded and reminds me that my work is never just for me, but for all of us.

And to the members of the Digital Stage community and the Digital Stage Academy, thank you. Your willingness to show up, share your stories and do the work is what makes this worth doing. This book exists because of the conversations we've had, the breakthroughs I've watched you make and the trust you've placed in me to be part of your journey. You are the reason I find this work genuinely rewarding.

INTRODUCTION

Have you ever hit record, stared into the lens, and suddenly forgotten how to be yourself?

You're not alone. Every day, countless brilliant people second-guess themselves the moment a camera appears. Experts, entrepreneurs, educators, leaders. People who are articulate, passionate and engaging in real life suddenly become stiff, self-conscious versions of themselves on screen.

It's not because they lack expertise. It's not because they don't have something valuable to share. And contrary to what most would believe, it's not because they lack confidence.

It's because they're caught in a story. A story about what confidence is supposed to look like, sound like, feel like. A story that says confidence is something you either have or don't. Something you must find, build, or fake.

This book challenges that story.

The Confidence Problem

We're living in an increasingly digital, video-driven world. From Zoom meetings to webinars, from social media to online courses, our ability to show up on camera has become inseparable from our ability to share our message, build our businesses and make an impact.

And yet, so many of us freeze. We procrastinate. We over-prepare. We record, delete and re-record until we're exhausted. Or worse, we don't record at all, watching opportunities pass us by because we're waiting to "feel ready."

The problem isn't a lack of tools or technology. It's not a lack of knowledge about what to say. The problem is how we think about confidence itself. We've been conditioned to believe that confidence is something you display rather than something you embody. We've confused performance with presence, polish with power. And in chasing the appearance of confidence, we've lost touch with the real thing.

The Promise of This Book

This book offers something different from the standard advice about camera confidence. I'm not going to give you a list of techniques to appear more confident. I'm not going to teach you how to fake it until you make it.

Instead, I'm going to help you rediscover the confidence you already have.

Confidence isn't something foreign to you. You've experienced it before, in conversations, in moments of flow, in situations where you were so connected to what you were sharing that you forgot to be self-conscious. That natural confidence exists. It's real. And it's available to you on camera too, not through more techniques or strategies, but through a fundamental shift in how you think about confidence itself.

By the end of this book, you'll have a completely different relationship with the camera. Not because you've learned to perform better, but because you've remembered how to be present. Not because you've mastered new skills, but because you've let go of old stories.

That shift is the confidence switch.

How to Use This Book

This isn't a traditional how-to manual. It's a journey of unlearning as much as it is of learning. Each chapter builds on the last, revealing a new aspect of true confidence and guiding you toward a more authentic, powerful presence on camera.

In each chapter, you'll find "Reality Check" sections that directly challenge common misconceptions about confidence. "The Shift" sections share real stories of transformation from my clients and my own journey. And "Flip the Switch" sections contain practical exercises to help you integrate each insight and embody your natural confidence on camera. I encourage you to write down your answers. The act of articulating your thoughts helps to cement new beliefs and perspectives. If you'd like a dedicated space to work through them, there's a free companion workbook available at confidenceswitch.com.

This book is designed to be both a journey and a reference. Read it from beginning to end to experience the full transformation, but feel free to return to specific chapters whenever you need a reminder or a reset.

The Journey Ahead

In the chapters that follow, we'll explore:

- Why the traditional concept of confidence is holding you back
- How the camera triggers familiar patterns of self-consciousness, and how to work with them

- Why perfectionism isn't your friend, but your biggest obstacle
- What real confidence actually feels like (hint: it's not what you think)
- The exact moment the confidence switch flips, and how to trigger it
- Practical techniques for speaking to one person through the lens
- How practice, not perfection, builds lasting confidence
- Ways to maintain your confidence once you've found it

By the end of this book, you won't just have strategies for looking more confident on camera. You'll have a fundamentally different relationship with confidence itself. You'll understand that confidence isn't something you find, build, or fake. It's something you remember. Something you return to. Something you allow.

And once you flip that switch, everything changes. Not just how you appear on camera, but how you show up in all areas of your life. True confidence isn't confined to video. It's a way of being that transforms every interaction, every message, every moment of impact.

So, let's begin. Not by becoming someone new, but by coming back to who you already are.

PART I

THE PROBLEM WE THINK WE HAVE

Most people assume the problem is simple, "I'm not confident on camera." So they go looking for techniques, scripts, lighting, better gear, more tips.

But what if confidence was never the thing you were missing?

In this first part, we're going to dismantle the common explanations and the familiar myths, the ones that make you believe the camera is the enemy and that you need to become a different version of yourself to show up well. We'll look at how the lens changes your attention, why you suddenly become self-aware, and why the harder you try to "look confident", the less confident you feel.

You don't need to fix yourself. You need to see the problem clearly.

Because once you do, the struggle starts to lose its grip.

1

THE CONFIDENCE MYTH

If you've ever said, "I'm not confident on camera," you're not alone. But most of us don't actually lack confidence. We just have the wrong idea of what confidence is.

We've been sold a version that looks a lot like performance: poised, polished, perfectly worded. No stumbles. No awkward pauses. No uncertainty. The kind of confidence you see in carefully edited TED talks, in news anchors who've been training for decades, in polished influencers who've recorded the same video twenty times before posting.

That's not confidence. That's acting.

The Performance Trap

When you step in front of a camera, you're not just sharing information. You're sharing yourself. And if you're carrying a mental image of what "confident" is supposed to look like, chances are it doesn't reflect your authentic self, even on your best day. It looks like some filtered version of a broadcaster, a TED speaker, or a YouTuber with ten years' experience.

So when you inevitably don't match that image, the story

kicks in: "I'm not good at this." "I don't sound professional enough." "I'll look silly." "I need to do another take... maybe twenty." And just like that, your natural presence, the thing people love about you in real life, starts to fade.

This performance-based idea of confidence creates an impossible standard. It says that to be confident, you need to eliminate all signs of humanity: the natural pauses, the occasional search for the right word, the genuine reactions that make communication real and relatable.

But think about the people who've most impacted you. The speakers, teachers or leaders whose words stayed with you long after they stopped talking. Were they perfect? Or were they present? Did they captivate you with flawless delivery, or with authentic conviction? In my experience, the moments that truly connect are rarely the most polished. They're the most present. The most real. The moments when someone stops trying to look confident and simply shares what matters to them.

The Control Illusion

What do we really mean when we say we're not confident? We might mean we feel awkward, unsure, exposed. But dig a little deeper and it's often about control. The kind of control we wish we had over how we appear to others. The kind of control that only exists in perfectly edited videos or highly curated feeds.

The trouble is that chasing control robs you of connection. It pulls your attention inward, toward your flaws, your filler words, your appearance, and away from the person you're actually trying to reach. When you're focused on controlling how you come across, you're essentially multitasking: delivering your message while simultaneously monitoring how you're delivering it. Your attention splits, which makes you less present, less articulate and, ironically, less confident.

Confidence, real confidence, doesn't come from control. It

comes from connection. From clarity. From choosing to focus on your message, not your image.

The Approval Addiction

I've seen incredibly powerful people shrink on camera, not because they weren't ready, but because they were aiming for the wrong target. They weren't aiming for impact. They were aiming for approval.

Here's a pattern I've noticed: the people who feel the least confident are often the ones who care the most. They care so deeply about their audience, their message, their reputation, that the stakes feel enormous. And when the stakes feel that high, we start to believe the only safe path is perfection. But perfection is a myth. And the pursuit of it is a trap.

If your goal is to create content that gets universal approval, that no one could possibly criticise or dislike, you've set yourself an impossible task. No message, no matter how carefully crafted, will resonate with everyone. And in trying to please everyone, you often end up connecting deeply with no one.

True confidence isn't about securing everyone's approval. It's about being at peace with the fact that not everyone will approve, and showing up anyway, because your message matters more than universal validation.

The True Nature of Confidence

Confidence, real confidence, isn't loud. It isn't flawless. It isn't polished. Confidence is presence. The ability to be with yourself in the moment, even if that moment is messy. The trust that your value doesn't evaporate the moment you misspeak or lose your train of thought. The strength to keep going even when your heart is racing or your hands are shaking.

It's not about eliminating the wobble. It's about learning to move with it.

This kind of confidence isn't a gift some people are born with and others miss out on. It's a skill. A way of seeing. You already have it. You've used it before. You've felt it in conversations, in leadership, in storytelling, in parenting, in friendships. You've had moments where you were so focused on what you were sharing, so connected to its value, that you forgot to be self-conscious. Those weren't flukes. Those were glimpses of your natural confidence.

You just haven't brought it fully into your relationship with the camera yet.

The High-Stakes Performer's Trap

Some of the most outwardly confident people struggle intensely with camera confidence. I've worked with high-level executives, experienced speakers and successful entrepreneurs who command rooms effortlessly in person but freeze the moment the camera turns on. One client, a CEO who regularly presented to rooms of hundreds, told me something revealing: "On stage, I'm sharing ideas. On camera, I feel like I'm exposing myself."

This captures something essential about the confidence myth. We've internalised the belief that being on camera is fundamentally different from other forms of communication, that it requires a different version of us. A more perfect version. A version that needs to be carefully controlled and curated.

But what if it doesn't? What if camera confidence is simply about transferring the natural presence you already have to this new medium? What if, instead of trying to become someone else on camera, you simply needed to remain yourself?

The Reframe That Changes Everything

If you've been stuck thinking, "I'm just not a confident person," I want to offer you a reframe. You don't need to become someone else. You just need to return to who you already are. Before the pressure, before the comparison, before the fear.

Confidence isn't something you earn once you're good enough. It's something that grows as you move, messily and imperfectly, through the moments that scare you. You'll still feel nervous sometimes. You'll still stumble. You'll still have moments of self-doubt. But the difference is this: you'll stop interpreting those things as evidence that you're not confident, and start seeing them as part of the path.

When It Happened to Me

I remember sitting in my home office, staring at the record button for what felt like the hundredth time that week. My palms were sweaty, my throat tight. Outside of recording, I could talk about these concepts for hours. I'd run live workshops with hundreds of people, feeling completely at ease. But the moment that camera light turned red, I became someone else. Stiff, scripted, second-guessing every word.

It made no sense to me. I could stand on a stage and hold a room without thinking twice about it. But put me in front of a lens with no audience, no feedback, no energy to read, and I fell apart. I'd spend hours, sometimes entire days, trying to record a simple ten-minute video. Take after take, deleted and restarted, convinced that the "perfect version" was just one more attempt away.

One particularly frustrating afternoon, after two hours of recording and re-recording a welcome video for a new course, I sat back and confronted an uncomfortable truth: I was trapped in the very performance mindset I've been describing in this chapter. I was so focused on appearing confident that I had lost my actual confidence.

That realisation was humbling, but it was also the beginning of something. I had to face the gap between who I was in a room and who I became in front of a camera. This book isn't written from the perspective of someone who was born "camera confident." It's written from the trenches, by someone who had to find his way back to natural presence one imperfect video at a time.

The principles in these pages aren't theoretical. They're the exact process I used to transform my relationship with the camera from anxiety to connection. The confidence switch I'm describing? I had to flip it myself first.

Reality Check: Confidence Isn't What You Think

MYTH #1: "Confident people never feel nervous."

Wrong. Confidence isn't the absence of nerves. It's the decision to move forward anyway. I've seen seasoned speakers who feel butterflies before every single session. The difference is they've learnt not to let that stop them. The physical sensations of anxiety and excitement are nearly identical. It's our interpretation that differs. Confident people don't eliminate nervousness. They reframe it as energy, as evidence that they care, as fuel for connection.

MYTH #2: "Confidence is something you're born with."

Absolutely not. Confidence is a skill, a habit. It's learnt. And like anything learnt, it gets stronger with practice, not with waiting. Every time you speak up, share your perspective or make yourself visible, the act itself becomes a little more familiar. That familiarity compounds. This is true regardless of your starting point.

MYTH #3: "You have to feel confident to be confident."

This one keeps more people stuck than anything else. Confidence often comes after you act, not before. It's a result, not a requirement. Think about learning to swim, to drive, to speak publicly. Did you feel fully confident before you did those things? Or did confidence grow as you practised them? Confidence is the reward for action, not the prerequisite.

MYTH #4: "Confidence means you never mess up."

In fact, truly confident people know they will mess up, and they trust themselves to handle it. That's what makes them look so grounded. I've seen speakers forget their lines, tech fail during presentations, webinars crash midway through. The ones who recover aren't those who never make mistakes. They're the ones who don't define themselves by their mistakes. A stumble doesn't erase your value.

*MYTH #5: "Looking confident
is the same as being confident."*

This is the big one. So many people are trying to project an image of confidence rather than building the foundation underneath. But a polished performance without presence will always feel hollow. Audiences are remarkably perceptive. They can sense when someone is performing confidence versus when someone is genuinely present. And they connect far more deeply with authentic presence than with perfect performance.

The Shift: The Most Confident Person in the Room

A few years ago, I was filming a promotional video with a friend I'll call Steven. He'd built and sold multiple businesses, some for eight figures. In any room he walked into, he was the most naturally commanding person there. He was sharp, decisive and warm in equal measure. The kind of leader people gravitate toward without quite knowing why.

We were shooting a short piece to promote an event where he was the headline. It should have been straightforward. He knew the material. He believed in the event. In conversation five minutes earlier, he'd explained the whole thing to me with effortless clarity.

Then the camera came on.

The ease disappeared. He'd start a take, stumble over a phrase he'd said perfectly moments before, and stop. We'd reset. He'd try again, get halfway through, then trail off. After each attempt, he'd turn to me with the same question: "How did that sound? Did that come across okay?"

This was a man who had negotiated deals worth more than most people will earn in a lifetime. He didn't need anyone's reassurance in a boardroom. But the moment a lens was pointed at him, he was looking to me for validation that he sounded all right.

We got there eventually. But what stayed with me wasn't the final take. It was that gap: the distance between who Steven was in conversation and who he became on camera. Nothing about his knowledge, experience or ability had changed. The only thing that changed was the story he was telling himself about what the camera demanded.

If confidence were simply a trait you either had or didn't, Steven would have had it on camera too. He had it everywhere else. But confidence doesn't work that way, and the camera has a way of proving it.

Flip the Switch: What's Your Definition?

Take a moment to pause and explore your current relationship with confidence.

Exercise 1: Your Confidence Definition

Write down your answer to this question: What does confidence mean to you right now? Don't edit yourself. Write whatever comes to mind first.

Exercise 2: Origin Story

Reflect on where that definition came from. Was it something you were taught explicitly? Observations of people you admire? Messages from media or social platforms? Past experiences of success or failure? Write down two or three specific influences that shaped your current definition.

Exercise 3: Impact Assessment

Complete these two sentences:
"My current definition of confidence helps me by..."
"My current definition of confidence limits me by..."
Look at what you've written. For most people, the second sentence reveals far more than the first.

Exercise 4: Definition Rewrite

Now, using what you've uncovered, create a new working definition. Even if it feels unfamiliar:
"Confidence is..."
Read this new definition aloud. Notice how it sits differently

from your original. You don't need to believe it fully yet. Just notice the difference.

Exercise 5: Make It Visible

Write your new definition somewhere you'll see it during your next recording session. A sticky note by your lens, a card on your desk, a reminder on your phone. Wherever it will meet you in the moment you need it most.

Let this be your starting point. You don't need a new version of yourself. You just need a new story.

And now that you have one, it's worth asking a different question. If confidence was never really the problem, what is? Most people have a ready answer: the camera. It makes them freeze, forget their words, become someone they don't recognise. But what if the camera isn't the problem either?

2

THE CAMERA IS NOT THE PROBLEM

I t's one of the most common things I hear from clients: "I'm fine in real life, but something happens when I'm on camera."

They're articulate, passionate and expressive in conversation. But then they hit record, and it's like a switch flips the wrong way. Their shoulders tense. Their voice goes flat. Their energy becomes mechanical. Natural gestures become awkward or disappear entirely. Thoughts that flowed effortlessly a moment ago suddenly scatter and fragment.

"I don't know what happened. I just didn't feel like me."

That feeling is more than frustrating. It can be disorienting. Because you know who you are. You know how you show up when you're fully present. But on camera, it feels like a different version of you has taken the wheel, and not the good kind.

The Camera as a Trigger

This isn't a flaw in you. It's a result of what the camera represents.

In real life, we get feedback. Nods. Smiles. Reactions. We

feel seen and heard. Communication is a dance between people: dynamic, responsive, alive. But on camera, there's silence. Stillness. A lens staring back. A void where human connection should be. And in that void, the mind rushes to fill the gap with stories. Stories about how we look, how we sound, what people will think. Stories about being judged, rejected, misunderstood.

It's not the camera that makes us freeze. It's what we imagine happening on the other side of it.

The Feedback Void

Think about how strange it is to pour your heart into a lens that doesn't respond. In conversation, we rely on subtle cues: eye contact, head nods, small affirmations like "mm-hmm" or "I see." We don't even realise how much we depend on that feed-back loop until it disappears. Our brains are wired for co-regulation, for the subtle adjustments of tone, pace and energy that happen in responsive interaction. When that regulation vanishes, we often default to our most mechanical, self-conscious versions.

And then come the layers of internal chatter: "Am I rambling?" "Do I look awkward?" "Why did I say it like that?" "Should I re-record?" The weight of being both the speaker and the imagined viewer is enormous. You're trying to deliver your message while simultaneously judging yourself from the outside. It's like trying to drive while constantly checking the rearview mirror. You lose track of where you're going because you're so focused on where you've been.

Suddenly, you're left with silence. And that silence becomes the breeding ground for anxiety. Instead of feeling like you're in connection, it feels like you're in performance. And performance, unless you're trained for it, rarely feels natural.

The Spotlight Effect

There's something else happening too. We dramatically overestimate how much others notice about us, especially our flaws and mistakes. While we might obsess over a stumble, a filler word or an awkward gesture, viewers are focused on the content and value of our message. They're not scrutinising us nearly as closely as we're scrutinising ourselves.

But when you're recording, that internal spotlight feels intense. You become hyper-aware of every detail: how your voice sounds, what your face is doing, whether you're speaking too fast or too slow. Things you'd never notice in natural conversation suddenly feel magnified. And this creates a loop: the more you notice, the more self-conscious you become. The more self-conscious you become, the less natural you appear. And the less natural you appear, the more you confirm your fear that you're "not good at this."

Here's what's really happening though. That shift is natural, and it's something you can work with. Your brain has formed an association: the lens equals threat, scrutiny, judgment. But that association isn't fixed. It can become something entirely different. A portal. A bridge to someone who needs exactly what you have to share.

The Portal Perspective

The key is presence. Anchoring yourself in the why instead of the how. The reason you hit record in the first place.

Why are you doing this? Who are you trying to help? What impact do you want to make? When you reconnect to those questions, something softens. Your tone shifts. Your body language relaxes. Your natural rhythm returns. You stop speaking at the camera and start speaking through it.

This isn't just a nice idea. It's a fundamental reframe that changes how your body responds. When you focus on service instead of performance, the threat response that tightens your chest and flattens your voice begins to ease. You move from self-protection into connection. And in that state, your natural expressiveness has room to return.

The question isn't "How do I look more confident on camera?" It's "How can I be more present with the person on the other side?" That shift in focus, from the camera as problem to the camera as portal, changes everything.

Building a New Association

You don't have to wait for the fear to go away before you start. You just have to stop letting it be the reason you don't.

Think about other technologies you've adapted to. Driving a car once felt awkward and overwhelming. Now you do it without conscious thought. Using a smartphone required your full attention. Now it's an extension of your hand. The first time you used video conferencing, it probably felt strange to see your own face while talking. Now it's routine.

The camera is no different. What feels foreign now can become familiar through repeated exposure and a shift in what the camera means to you. It won't happen instantly. But it will happen if you keep showing up, not to perform, but to connect. Your hands stop shaking. Your breathing evens out. You find your words more easily. And then one day, you'll record a video and realise you actually enjoyed it. That's not magic. That's practice. That's presence. That's confidence taking root.

Because the moment you change what the camera means to you, you change how you show up in front of it. Instead of seeing it as an evaluator capturing your flaws, start seeing it as a conduit: a tool that allows your message to reach precisely the people who need it. When you shift your focus from "how do I look?" to "who am I helping?", you move from self-conscious-ness into service. And those two states simply cannot coexist.

This doesn't mean you won't still feel nervous sometimes. It means you'll recognise that nervousness isn't the problem, and it certainly isn't evidence that you're not cut out for video. It simply means you care about making an impact. And caring is the foundation of authentic communication.

Reality Check: The Camera Isn't the Problem

MYTH #1: "The camera makes me nervous."

The camera itself is neutral. It's a piece of glass and metal. What triggers anxiety is your interpretation of what being on camera means: what it will say about you, how others will judge you, what could go wrong. Some people feel perfectly comfortable on camera. The same technology that triggers anxiety for one person is simply a tool for another. The difference isn't in the camera. It's in the meaning you've assigned to it.

*MYTH #2: "I just don't have
a good camera presence."*

There's no such thing as a "camera person." There are just people who've learnt to relax and connect through a lens. That's a skill, not a trait. Some people have had more practice or different conditioning, but the capacity to develop camera confidence exists in everyone. If you can connect with another human being in conversation, you can learn to do it through a camera.

MYTH #3: "It feels fake to speak to a machine."

It does feel fake at first. That's not a flaw in you. It's a normal response to an unfamiliar medium. But over time, it becomes second nature. Think about how strange it once felt to talk on the telephone, a technology we now use without thinking. The camera follows the same curve. What feels mechanical today can become invisible with practice, especially once you start picturing a real person behind the lens instead of an empty void.

MYTH #4: *"People will notice every mistake I make."*

They won't. We consistently overestimate how much others notice our flaws and mistakes. While you might obsess over a stumble or a filler word, viewers are focused on whether your content helps them. They're looking for solutions, insights and connection, not scrutinising your every gesture. The mistakes that feel enormous to you are usually invisible to them.

MYTH #5: *"I need to become a different person on camera."*

This might be the most damaging myth of all. The most engaging people on camera are the ones who bring their authentic selves to the lens. They aren't trying to become someone else. They're simply translating their natural presence to a new medium. Your goal isn't to create a "camera version" of yourself. It's to be fully yourself, through the camera.

The Shift: The Window, Not the Mirror

A client I'll call Jill came to me because she was struggling with her on-camera presence. She ran online workshops regularly and was good at what she did, but something kept pulling her out of the room.

It came up almost in passing. "I keep getting distracted," she said. "I'm supposed to be delivering a training, but I'm watching myself the whole time. I'm editing my posture while I'm speaking. I'm checking whether I look friendly enough, enthusiastic enough. I catch a glimpse of my own expression and think, does that look confident? And then I've lost three sentences of my own material because I wasn't paying attention to what I was saying."

She wasn't struggling with her content. She wasn't struggling with the technology. She was struggling with the fact that Zoom was giving her a live feed of herself while she was trying to connect with other people. Every call came with a mirror she never asked for, and she couldn't stop looking into it.

The fix was remarkably simple. Before her next workshop, she hid her self-view in Zoom. One click. The little rectangle of her own face disappeared, and all that was left on her screen were the people she was actually there to speak to.

When she reported back afterwards, the difference surprised even her. She'd been more present than she could remember being in any online session. She'd noticed people's reactions in real time, responded to their energy, adjusted her pace naturally. Not because she'd learned a new technique, but because she'd removed the thing that had been pulling her away from the conversation all along.

The camera hadn't been the problem. It never was. The problem was what she'd been using it to do: watch herself instead of connecting with the people on the other side.

Flip the Switch: What Does The Camera Mean To You?

Let's explore your current relationship with the camera and begin shifting it into something more useful.

Exercise 1: Emotional Inventory

Write down the first three to five emotions that come up when you see a camera lens pointed at you. Be honest. These emotions aren't permanent, and naming them is the first step to changing them.

Exercise 2: Expectation Examination

Complete this sentence with as much specific detail as you can:
"When I'm on camera, I feel I need to..."
Now look at what you've written. Would you place these same expectations on a friend? Are they realistic? Are they even necessary for effective communication?

Exercise 3: Purpose Reconnection

Write your answer to this question: What's the real reason you want to create content?
Not the metrics. Not the business goals. What impact do you actually hope to make in someone's life? Keep this answer somewhere visible. It's the antidote to self-consciousness.

Exercise 4: Relationship Reframe

Imagine the camera as a person. Which of these would it be?

- A critical judge evaluating your performance

- A distant stranger watching with indifference
- A supportive friend eager to help share your message
- A bridge connecting you to someone who needs what you offer

Now, deliberately choose a new relationship. Write: "From now on, my camera represents..."

Exercise 5: Make It Physical

Take what you wrote in Exercise 4 and put it somewhere you'll see it when you record. A sticky note by your lens, a card on your desk, whatever works. Before you hit record next time, read it. Let it reset how you relate to the lens before you speak a word.

Because once you change the story about what the camera is, you stop becoming someone else in front of it. You just show up as you.

And that raises a deeper question. If the camera isn't really the problem, and your idea of confidence isn't really the problem, what is? For many of us, the answer is something we'd rather not look at directly. It's not the fear of the camera at all. It's the fear of being seen.

3

THE FEAR OF BEING SEEN

Y ou might think your fear is about the camera. But what if it's actually about being seen? Really seen. Not just your words. Not just your content. You. Your quirks. Your pauses. Your voice. Your truth.

There's a vulnerability to that. And for many of us, that's the real discomfort. We're not afraid of the lens. We're afraid of what being seen through that lens might mean.

The Vulnerability Paradox

In everyday life, we present ourselves in layers. We adjust depending on who we're with, where we are, how safe we feel. We have subtle control over how much of ourselves we reveal in any given interaction.

But when you speak to a camera, you don't know exactly who's watching. There's no feedback, no signals of safety. It feels like walking into a room with every light pointed at you and none of the people visible. And in that spotlight, the brain goes into defence mode: "What if I mess up?" "What if they think I'm not good enough?" "What if they see the parts of me I've worked so hard to hide?"

This is the vulnerability paradox. The very thing that makes content powerful, authentic human connection, is the thing that feels most frightening to offer. We know intuitively that vulnerability builds trust. We're drawn to people who show their humanity. And yet, when it's our turn to be vulnerable, we freeze. We hide. We polish away the very qualities that would make our message resonate.

The Ancient Wiring

That fear is ancient. It goes back to something primal: the fear of rejection. The fear of exclusion from the group. In our evolutionary past, being cast out meant danger, isolation, even death. So our nervous system treats judgment, or even the possibility of judgment, as a threat. And the camera triggers that possibility every time.

When you hit record, you're creating something permanent. Something that could be viewed by anyone, at any time, in any context. Something beyond your direct control. For the part of your brain still wired for tribal survival, that registers as risk. And risk triggers protection: holding back, speaking carefully, abandoning authenticity in favour of what feels "safe."

But those protection mechanisms create the very disconnection you're afraid of. By trying to look perfect, you become less relatable. By polishing away your humanity, you lose the thing that creates trust.

The Stories We Carry

Many of us carry old stories. Maybe you were laughed at in school. Told you were too much, or not enough. Maybe someone mocked your voice, your laugh, your accent. You might not consciously think about those moments anymore. But they live in your body. They resurface the moment you step into the spotlight.

Visibility becomes associated with shame. And to stay "safe," we avoid being fully seen. We edit. We script. We hide behind graphics and gear. I see this pattern constantly in my work. A client who's naturally expressive becomes rigid on camera. A brilliant storyteller suddenly speaks in bullet points. A visionary leader starts using corporate jargon instead of the passionate language that inspires in person.

These aren't conscious choices. They're protective responses, attempts to minimise the perceived risk of being truly seen. But the price of that safety is disconnection. From your message. From your audience. From yourself.

The Service Reframe

What if being seen isn't a threat, but a service?

What if your willingness to show up, with all your imperfections, gives someone else permission to do the same? What if your presence is the exact message someone needs, not in spite of your vulnerability, but because of it?

Every time you choose to be visible, you model courage. You demonstrate leadership. You shift what's possible for someone else. That's the true power of presence. I've seen this repeatedly in my own journey and in the journeys of my clients. The videos that get the most response, the most gratitude, the most impact, they're rarely the most polished. They're the most human.

A client once told me about a video she almost didn't post because she got emotional while recording it. She decided to share it anyway, without editing out the moment her voice cracked. The response was dozens of messages from people saying, "This was exactly what I needed to hear," and "Thank you for being so real." Her vulnerability wasn't a weakness. It was a gift.

The Visibility Myth

Part of our discomfort with being seen comes from a fundamental misunderstanding. We believe visibility should be earned, that we need to reach some threshold of excellence or success before we deserve to take up space. But that's backwards.

Visibility isn't a reward for perfection. It's not something you qualify for once you've ticked enough boxes. The real question isn't "Have I earned the right to be visible?" It's "What happens if I withhold my message from people who might benefit from it?"

If the fear of being seen feels strong for you, that's not a sign of weakness. It's a sign of investment. You care. You want your message to land. You want your work to matter. Let that caring fuel your courage, not your self-censorship.

Because the moment you step into the discomfort of being seen, something starts to shift. You begin to reclaim your voice. You begin to dismantle the story that says you have to hide. You begin to build the muscle of showing up. And slowly, you start to trust that who you are is not only enough, but exactly what's needed.

Reality Check: Visibility Isn't Threatening

MYTH #1: "If people really saw me, they'd reject me."

Most people aren't looking for perfection. They're looking for something real. Authentic presence builds connection, not rejection. We're drawn to people who show their humanity. This doesn't mean sharing everything or abandoning boundaries. It means being genuine: allowing your natural warmth, your occasional imperfection and your real personality to come through.

MYTH #2: "It's safer to hide behind the brand, the script, or the gear."

Those tools can support you, but they can't replace you. People trust people, not polish. Think about your own experience as a viewer. Do you connect more with slick, corporate content, or with real people sharing valuable insights in their own voice? Even at the highest levels, the creators and leaders who build lasting trust are the ones who let themselves be seen.

MYTH #3: "I have to be fully confident before I can show up."

You don't have to have it all figured out before you can be present. Some of the most powerful voices in any industry share their journeys in real time. They don't wait until they've "arrived" to start helping others along the path. Their willingness to be visible while still growing is precisely what makes people trust them.

MYTH #4: "Vulnerability means oversharing or being unprofessional."

There's a difference between strategic vulnerability and inappropriate disclosure. Being real within professional boundaries might look like acknowledging when you don't know something, sharing a relevant personal story that illuminates a point, or showing genuine emotion about something that matters to you. That's not unprofessional. It's the opposite of the distant, guarded style that actually creates barriers to trust.

MYTH #5: "I need to look successful before I can be visible."

Success follows visibility, not the other way around. The creators and leaders you admire didn't wait until they were polished to start sharing. Their willingness to be visible was part of what created their success. Their growth, shared openly, deepened the connection their audience felt with them. Waiting until you've "made it" means waiting to start the very thing that gets you there.

The Shift: The Coach Who Kept the Door Closed

A client I'll call Sarah was a business coach who helped entrepreneurs turn struggling businesses around. She was good at it, and for a reason her audience didn't know: she'd been through it herself. Years earlier, a business she'd built had failed. Not quietly. The kind of failure that takes everything with it for a while.

That experience was the foundation of everything she taught. It gave her work its edge and her advice its honesty. In one-to-one sessions, she shared it openly. Clients found it reassuring. Here was someone who'd actually been where they were, not just someone with a framework and a qualification.

But on camera, the door closed. Her content was polished, professional and carefully impersonal. She shared strategies, structures and practical steps. She never shared why she knew they worked. Because a video isn't a private conversation. A video lives on the internet, visible to anyone: future clients, peers, people from her old industry who remembered what happened. The camera took a story she could control in a private room and made it permanent and public. That was the part she couldn't get past.

When I asked her about it, she was direct. People were trusting her to help them save their businesses. If they knew hers had failed, why would they listen?

I asked her to try it once. One piece of content where she told the truth about where her expertise actually came from.

The response was immediate. People thanked her for saying what most business coaches wouldn't. They told her it was the first time they'd felt genuinely understood by someone in her position. The thing she'd been protecting them from turned out to be the thing they'd been looking for.

And that changed her relationship with the camera entirely.

Once she realised that being seen didn't lead to judgment but to connection, the resistance that had kept her from recording started to fall away. The camera was no longer the place where she might be exposed. It became the place where she could finally be honest.

Flip the Switch: Rewriting The Visibility Story

These questions go deeper than the previous exercises. Take your time with them.

Exercise 1: The Origin

When did you first learn that being seen was risky? Think back to early experiences where you felt vulnerable being visible. A class presentation gone wrong. A moment of being laughed at. Critical feedback from a parent or teacher. You don't need to relive these moments in detail, but understanding them can help you see how your current relationship with visibility was shaped.

Exercise 2: The Fear Behind the Fear

What are you actually afraid people will think if they really see you? Get specific. Are you afraid of being judged as unprofessional? Not smart enough? Too emotional? Too opinionated? Write them down. Naming these fears doesn't make them bigger. It usually makes them smaller.

Exercise 3: The Cost of Hiding

What part of yourself are you tired of hiding? We all have aspects of ourselves we've learnt to downplay or conceal. But hiding takes energy, energy that could be directed toward connection and impact. What qualities, stories or experiences might actually strengthen your message if you allowed them to be seen?

Exercise 4: The New Story

Complete this sentence:

"Being seen is safe because..."

Here are some examples to get you started:

"Being seen is safe because my value doesn't depend on universal approval."

"Being seen is safe because my imperfections create connection, not rejection."

"Being seen is safe because I trust myself to handle whatever happens."

Write your own version. Say it out loud. And repeat it every time you hit record.

The more you practise showing up, even in the presence of fear, the less power that fear holds over you. You're not afraid of the camera. You never were. You're afraid of being seen. And now you know you can handle it.

That's the real shift. Not learning a new skill, not becoming someone different, but recognising that the problem was never what you thought it was.

INTEGRATING PART ONE

From Myth to Clarity

In the first three chapters, you've looked at the problem differently. Not "What's wrong with me?" but "What am I making the camera mean?"

You've seen three core truths:

- Confidence isn't performance. It's presence.
- The camera isn't the trigger. It's the meaning you attach to it.
- The fear of being seen is common, and it can be redirected into service.

Before you move on, take a moment to reflect:

Which belief about being on camera are you ready to let go of? And what would change if you treated the camera as a point of connection rather than a source of judgement?

Carry this forward: what you've been experiencing isn't a confidence problem. It's a framing problem.

PART II

THE STORY THAT BEGINS TO UNRAVEL

There comes a moment where the whole thing starts to make sense.

Not in a motivational way. In a practical way. You realise the issue was never a lack of confidence, it was a misunderstanding of what confidence is.

In this part, we'll make the central shift. We'll move from performance to presence, from trying to manage an image to focusing on a person. You'll start to notice what changes when your attention moves outward again, and why "being yourself on camera" isn't something you force, it's something you return to.

This is where the story begins to unravel.

And once it does, it's very hard to go back to the old way of thinking.

4

THE ILLUSION OF PERFECTION

Perfectionism is a word we hear all the time. It sounds harmless, even admirable. Who wouldn't want things to be "just right"? Isn't that a sign of high standards?

But let's get honest about what perfectionism actually does, especially when it comes to being on camera. It stalls you. It silences you. It keeps you endlessly tweaking and re-recording and rewriting because nothing ever feels quite good enough. It transforms what should be a tool for connection into an exhausting exercise in self-criticism.

I know, because I've been there.

The Perfection Trap

Before Take One Tech, before I fully embraced a live, one-take workflow, I was stuck in that loop. I would spend days, sometimes weeks, trying to record a single video. Ten minutes of content would balloon into hours of second-guessing, editing, redoing, overanalysing. It was exhausting. And I always told myself it was because I wanted it to be perfect. I wanted it to be professional. I wanted to do my audience justice.

But if I go one level deeper, here's what I now understand: I wasn't trying to be perfect. I was trying to look confident. I thought that if I could eliminate every stumble, every pause, every imperfect sentence, then people would see me as someone who had it all together. Someone worth listening to. Someone credible.

But the pursuit of "looking confident" was actually eroding my real confidence. With every retake, I was reinforcing the belief that I wasn't good enough as I was. That natural delivery wasn't trustworthy. That the first take was never acceptable. That I needed to be fixed before I could be seen.

And the irony? The more I tried to control how I came across, the less connected I became to the message itself.

The Image Illusion

This is what perfectionism does. It shifts your focus from impact to image, from service to self-consciousness, from presence to performance. It tells you that your value lies in flawlessness, not in authenticity. That what matters most is how you appear, not what you contribute.

And the more you chase the illusion of perfection, the more elusive confidence becomes. Because perfectionism is not just about getting things right. It's about the fear of being wrong. It's a defence mechanism dressed up as diligence. It gives you an excuse to delay, an excuse to hide, a reason not to risk being seen in your messiness. And it whispers the same lie, again and again: "If you're not perfect, you'll be rejected." "If you mess up, people will stop listening." "If you show weakness, they won't trust you."

But what if none of that is true?

The Trust Dynamic

What if people actually crave realness? What if the occasional stumble or pause makes you more relatable? What if the trust you're trying to earn is already there, but you're covering it up by trying too hard?

There's a reason the most powerful content often feels unscripted. It's not because people admire imperfection for its own sake. It's because imperfection signals humanity. And humanity builds trust.

The very flaws you're trying to eliminate might be the doorway to deeper connection. When you watch someone who's clearly reading from a script, whose delivery is flawless, you don't feel connected to them. You feel like you're watching a performance. But when someone speaks naturally, occasionally pauses to find the right word, or laughs at themselves when they misspeak, you're drawn in. You trust what they're saying more, not less.

Perfection creates distance. Humanity creates connection.

The High Stakes of "Getting It Right"

Perfectionism isn't just about wanting things to be excellent. It's about tying your worth to your performance. It's about believing that if you get it "wrong," something terrible will happen.

For most of us, this isn't a conscious belief. But it drives our behaviour nonetheless. We procrastinate on creating videos because we're afraid they won't be good enough. We record and re-record until we're exhausted. We focus on all the ways we fell short instead of the value we provided.

This high-stakes mindset turns what could be a joyful act of sharing into a high-pressure performance. And under that kind of pressure, natural presence is the first thing to go.

But what if you could lower the stakes? What if a single video wasn't a measure of your worth, your expertise, or your future success? What if it was just a video?

The Permission Breakthrough

Here's what changed everything for me: I let go of the idea that confidence had to look a certain way. I stopped trying to "get it right." I committed to showing up as I am.

And in doing that, something shifted. I started connecting more deeply with my audience. I started enjoying the process. I started trusting myself. Confidence wasn't waiting at the end of perfection. It was waiting at the end of permission, the moment I gave myself permission to be real.

This is a pattern I've seen repeated with hundreds of clients. The moment they stop trying to be perfect, they start being present. And presence is what creates connection.

The Sincerity Solution

You don't need to chase perfection to be taken seriously. You need to show up with sincerity.

Sincerity isn't about being flawless. It's about being transparent, letting people see that you genuinely care about the message you're sharing and the people you're sharing it with. And here's the thing: sincerity requires far less effort than perfection. You don't have to manufacture it. You don't have to rehearse it. You just have to stop hiding it behind a mask of polish and performance.

If you've been stuck in the trap of trying to look confident, trying to edit yourself into perfection, this is your invitation to stop. You don't need to earn your place on camera by getting everything right. You earn it by showing up. And the more you do, the more you'll see: your imperfect presence is more powerful than your polished performance.

Reality Check: Perfectionism Isn't Professionalism

MYTH #1: "If it's not perfect, it's not professional."

Think about the most respected leaders, educators and creators in your field. Are they flawless? Or are they genuine? The most engaging people on camera are the ones who let their realness show. Professionalism isn't about eliminating every rough edge. It's about providing consistent value with integrity, and you can do that without being perfect.

MYTH #2: "If I make a mistake, I'll lose credibility."

The opposite is usually true. Making a mistake and recovering gracefully shows you're human, adaptable and not hiding behind a script. People who appear competent but occasionally stumble tend to come across as more relatable and trustworthy than those who seem impossibly polished. A small mistake humanises you without diminishing your expertise.

MYTH #3: "I just want to do my audience justice."

That instinct is good, but follow it to its conclusion. If you have something valuable to share and you never share it because the delivery isn't perfect, you're not doing your audience justice at all. They'd rather hear an imperfect message that helps them than a perfect one that never arrives.

MYTH #4: *"I'll feel more confident once I get it right."*

Every creator I know who appears effortlessly confident on camera got there through consistent action, not through perfection. They recorded when they were nervous. They published when it wasn't quite right. They prioritised showing up over getting it polished. Confidence doesn't arrive once you've nailed the perfect take. It builds through repetition.

MYTH #5: *"Perfect content performs better."*

Not according to the people actually watching. Authentic, value-driven content consistently outperforms overly polished content, especially for creators, educators and entrepreneurs. Your audience isn't looking for a television presenter. They're looking for someone they can trust to help them solve a problem or reach a goal.

The Shift: The Course That Almost Never Happened

I once worked with a brilliant educator who'd been trying to create her first online course for the best part of a year. In a live room, she was magnetic. She could hold an audience's attention for hours, explain complex ideas with clarity and warmth, and make every person in the room feel like she was speaking directly to them.

But the moment she sat down to record the course, everything stalled. She didn't feel enthused. She didn't feel ready. She'd script a module, record it, watch it back, delete it. The version of herself on screen didn't match the version her live audiences knew. She sounded flat, overly careful, like she was reading something rather than sharing something. Months passed. The course remained unfinished.

The breakthrough came sideways. Rather than trying to record another polished module, she decided to deliver the material live over Zoom to a real audience and record the session. The setup was physically identical to her failed recording attempts — the same camera, the same room, the same screen. The only difference was that there were real people on the other side of it.

The recording was imperfect. There were tangents and pauses and moments where she lost her thread and found it again. But it sounded like her. It had the energy, the clarity and the warmth that her scripted takes had been missing. She used that recording as the course.

The feedback from her students was extraordinary. They commented specifically on how engaging and authentic she was, how it felt like she was right there in the room with them. Not a single person mentioned the production quality.

But the real shift was what happened next. Once she saw what worked, she realised she could record pre-recorded content the same way. Same camera, same room, no audience — but speaking as if someone were right there with her. The perfectionism hadn't been protecting her standards. It had been preventing her from doing the thing she was already good at.

Flip the Switch: What Would "Good Enough" Look Like?

These exercises are designed to help you notice where perfectionism is running the show and what happens when you loosen its grip.

Exercise 1: Name the Pattern

Think about the last piece of content you delayed, re-recorded or never published. What was the reason you gave yourself at the time? Now look at that reason again. Was it genuinely about quality, or was it about how you'd be perceived? Most perfectionist stalling has a fear of judgement underneath it, not a real quality problem. Naming the pattern is the first step to loosening its grip.

Exercise 2: The Real Risk

Pick one piece of content you've been holding back. Ask yourself: what is the actual, realistic consequence of publishing it as it is? Not the catastrophic version your fear invents, but the likely one. Then ask the opposite question: what is the cost of continuing to wait? The opportunities, the connections, the people who could have been helped. Most of the time, the cost of waiting far outweighs the risk of imperfection.

Exercise 3: Define Your "Good Enough"

Finish this sentence in your own words: "My content is good enough when..." Make it specific to you. It might be something like "when I've clearly shared the core idea" or "when it would genuinely help the person watching." Whatever your version is, write it down somewhere you'll see it. This becomes your standard, and it replaces the impossible one perfectionism has been holding you to.

Exercise 4: Record and Release

Choose a topic you know well. Record a short video in one take, no longer than two minutes. Don't watch it back. Post it, send it to someone, or save it to a shared folder. The point isn't the content itself. It's the act of letting something exist without editing it into submission. Notice what comes up when you do this, and notice what happens when the world doesn't end.

Once you stop demanding perfection from yourself, something opens up. Not just more time or less stress, but a question that's worth sitting with: if confidence was never about getting it right, what is it actually about?

That's where we're going next.

5

WHAT CONFIDENCE REALLY IS

So if confidence isn't about getting it right, what is it really? Confidence is trust.

It's not loud or flashy. It's not an act. It's the quiet, grounded knowing that you can handle whatever happens. It's what allows you to show up even when things aren't perfect, to speak even when your voice shakes, and to be seen without shrinking back or trying to control how you're perceived.

The Presence Principle

Think about the people who've impacted you the most. The voices you've trusted. The stories that stayed with you. Chances are, they weren't the most polished or rehearsed. They were present. They were real. They weren't trying to impress you. They were trying to reach you. That's what real confidence looks like.

It's not a skill you earn. It's a space you return to.

We all have that space. But we forget it when we start chasing some external ideal of what we're supposed to sound or look like. We trade presence for performance, and then wonder why we feel disconnected.

Presence is the foundation of confidence. When you're fully present, connected to your message, aware of your audience and grounded in your purpose, you access a natural authority that no amount of polish can manufacture. Your breath deepens. Your voice settles. Your gestures become more natural. You become more you.

The Confidence Paradox

Confidence isn't some mystical quality reserved for a few charismatic people. It's a mindset. A habit of showing up fully. A willingness to be seen without the need to be perfect.

And it can grow without you even realising it. Every time you speak up in a meeting when you're unsure. Every time you hit record when you're feeling nervous. Every time you share an idea, post a video, teach a lesson or tell a story, you're reinforcing a powerful internal message: "I trust myself."

That trust is the foundation. It doesn't mean you won't doubt yourself sometimes. It doesn't mean you won't make mistakes. But it means you won't crumble when things go sideways. You'll breathe, regroup and continue.

This is the confidence paradox: confidence isn't the absence of doubt. It's the willingness to coexist with doubt without being ruled by it. It's not about eliminating uncertainty. It's about developing a relationship with uncertainty that allows you to move forward anyway.

The most confident people I know aren't free from self-doubt. They simply don't let that doubt have the final say in their decisions. They recognise it as a normal part of growth, not a sign that something's wrong.

The Courage Prerequisite

Confidence is the willingness to continue. To stay in the game. To speak, even if you shake. To lead, even when you question your readiness.

But here's something crucial: confidence often looks like courage first.

Courage is what happens when you act despite your fear, when you show up despite your doubts, when you hit record even though your heart is racing. And there's a sequence to how it works. Courage leads to action. Action creates evidence. Evidence builds trust. And trust becomes confidence.

You don't overcome fear first and then take action. You take action first, and in doing so, you build the evidence that gradually transforms fear into trust. This is why waiting to "feel confident" before you start creating content is a trap. The feeling rarely comes first. It follows action, not the other way around.

The Internal Trust Shift

Another critical shift in developing genuine confidence is moving from external validation to internal trust. When your sense of "doing well" depends entirely on how others respond, you'll always feel shaky. Because you can't control how others receive your content. You can only control how present you are in creating it.

True confidence comes from developing internal markers of success. Did I show up fully? Did I share what I genuinely believe to be valuable? Did I stay present? Did I honour my own voice? These are things you can actually control. And when you start measuring success this way, you free yourself from the emotional rollercoaster of external validation.

This doesn't mean feedback isn't valuable. It absolutely is. But there's a difference between learning from feedback and deriving your entire sense of worth from it. Internal trust says: "I value the response of my audience, but my worth isn't determined by it. I trust myself to keep showing up and keep learning, regardless of any single outcome."

The Service Mindset

Here's what happens when you stop trying to look confident: you actually start to look confident. Because your focus shifts from you to your message.

You stop thinking "Do I sound smart enough?" and "Do I look OK?" and you start thinking "How can I help the person watching this?" and "What do they need to hear?" That shift in attention changes everything. The internal friction that comes from monitoring your own performance disappears. You flow. You connect. You embody the very confidence you've been chasing.

This isn't just a nice idea. It's a practical tool for accessing your natural confidence. Next time you feel self-conscious on camera, ask yourself: "Who am I here to help, and how can I best help them?" Notice how that question shifts your energy from self-focused anxiety to something far more useful.

The Feel of Real Confidence

Confidence doesn't always feel like confidence.

It often feels like courage. It feels like vulnerability. It feels like pushing through the resistance and doing it anyway. It feels like sitting down to record a video when you'd rather wait, or publishing a post even though it's not perfect, or trusting that showing up as you are is enough. Because it is.

Confidence isn't the absence of fear. It's the presence of commitment. The commitment to keep going, to keep speaking, to keep telling the truth.

Many of my clients are surprised when I tell them that I still feel nervous before recording sometimes. After years of creating content and coaching others, you might expect the nerves to disappear completely. But they don't. They just stop running the show.

I've learned to recognise nervousness as energy, as evidence that I care, as a signal that I'm stretching beyond comfort into growth. And in reframing it that way, the nervousness loses its power to stop me.

That's what real confidence is. Not the absence of discomfort, but the ability to move with it rather than be stopped by it.

So the next time you feel that inner pressure rise, that urge to perform or impress or be perfect, pause. Take a breath. Remember who you are. And remember who you're speaking to.

Confidence lives in that space.

Reality Check: Confidence Isn't Performance

*MYTH #1: "Confidence means
always knowing what to say."*

Confidence means being okay even when you don't know what to say. It means being present enough to listen, adjust and speak honestly. Some of the most powerful moments in communication happen when someone says "I don't know, but here's what I'm thinking." Real confidence includes the humility to acknowledge your limits and the security to be honest about them.

*MYTH #2: "Confident people
don't care what others think."*

Confident people care deeply. They're just not ruled by it. They care more about what they're here to do than how they're perceived doing it. There's a world of difference between being indifferent to others and being independent of their approval. Confident people aren't aloof. They're centred. They can consider feedback without being devastated by criticism.

MYTH #3: "Confidence is a fixed trait."

Confidence is contextual. You can feel confident in one area and shaky in another, and that's completely normal. I know brilliant physicians who freeze when asked to record a simple video. I know natural performers who get anxious making business decisions. Acknowledging that confidence is situational removes the pressure to perform it as though it were a permanent personality trait.

MYTH #4: "Confidence comes from being impressive."

The most compelling speakers are often the ones who feel like they're sitting right next to you, not above you. Connection outshines charisma every time. True confidence doesn't try to create distance or hierarchy. It brings you alongside your audience. The most confident communicators make complex ideas accessible and speak with clarity rather than complexity.

MYTH #5: "Confidence feels like certainty."

This might be the most limiting belief of all. Confidence often coexists with uncertainty. It's not about feeling sure of yourself. It's about being willing to move forward even when you don't. Waiting for complete certainty before you act is a recipe for paralysis. Real confidence embraces the reality that growth requires stepping into the unknown.

The Shift: The Day Confidence Showed Up Differently

I produce and host the Digital Stage Summit, an annual three-day virtual event. Forty-two speakers, commentators and panellists across eleven hours a day. I run it essentially as a one-man production: hosting, producing, managing the tech and keeping everything on schedule.

On the first day of the inaugural event, things went wrong. The stream dropped. Not a small glitch. The whole thing stopped. I had an audience watching, speakers lined up, and a live broadcast that had just gone dark.

In that moment, I didn't think about confidence. I didn't think about how I looked or sounded or whether people were judging me. I restarted the stream, posted a link in the original broadcast so people could find the new one, communicated what was happening, and got us back on track. There were a few more technical problems that morning, and each time the same thing happened: something broke, I fixed it, we moved on.

Afterwards, someone sent me a message that stopped me in my tracks. "You looked so confident handling all of that." And I remember thinking: I didn't feel confident. I wasn't standing there radiating calm self-assurance. I was problem-solving in real time with no script and no safety net. But that, it turned out, was exactly what confidence looked like.

It wasn't a feeling I'd summoned before the event. It wasn't preparation or polish. It was trust. Trust that I could handle whatever came up, even when I didn't know what was coming. I also knew, from experience, that the audience wasn't hoping I'd fail. The vast majority of people watching were rooting for me to get it back on track. And that knowledge was part of the trust too.

That day changed how I understood confidence entirely. It's not always knowing what to say and do. Sometimes it's knowing you'll find a way forward when you don't know what to say and do. That quiet trust was always there. I just hadn't recognised it as confidence until someone pointed it out.

Flip the Switch: Defining Confidence For Yourself

These exercises help you step back from what confidence is supposed to look like and start working with what it actually means to you.

Exercise 1: Your Personal Confidence Definition

Complete this sentence in writing: "To me, confidence means..." Don't think about it too long. Write the first honest answer that comes. Then read it aloud. Notice how it feels to claim your own definition rather than borrowing someone else's.

Exercise 2: Confidence Mapping

On a piece of paper, create two columns. In the first, list three to five situations where you already feel naturally confident. In the second, identify what allows that confidence to emerge in each one. Is it familiarity? Purpose? Preparation? Connection to the people involved? Look for the patterns. They'll tell you something useful about what confidence actually needs from you.

Exercise 3: The Confidence Bridge

Choose one upcoming content creation opportunity: a video, a presentation, a meeting. Look at your patterns from Exercise 2 and write down specifically how you could bring those same conditions into this context. If familiarity is what supports your confidence, how could you create more of it before you record? If purpose is what grounds you, how could you reconnect with your "why" before you hit the button?

Exercise 4: The Confidence Reminder

Write a short phrase that captures your definition of confidence from Exercise 1. Put it on a sticky note near your camera or workspace. Before you record, read it. Let it remind you of what confidence actually means to you, not what you've been told it should look like.

Confidence doesn't start with how you perform. It starts with what you believe. And something in that belief is already beginning to shift.

8

PRESENCE OVER PERFORMANCE

Something begins to change when you stop thinking of confidence as a performance and start experiencing it as a way of being. But there's a gap between understanding that idea and actually feeling it in your body, your voice, your presence on camera.

This chapter is about closing that gap. Not with more techniques to master, but by reconnecting with something you already do naturally when you're not trying to perform.

The Physical Experience of Presence

There's a fundamental difference between showing up and showing off. Between being present and performing. Performance is about how you look. Presence is about how you connect. And that difference isn't just mental. It's physical.

You've experienced this in everyday life. Those moments when you're so absorbed in a conversation that you forget to be self-conscious. When you're sharing a story you care about and time seems to disappear. When you're teaching something you know deeply and the words just come.

In those moments, your body relaxes. Your breathing deepens. Your gestures become more fluid. Your voice carries more warmth and variation. You're not thinking about how you look. You're fully in the moment, and it shows.

This is what presence feels like in the body. And it's immediately perceptible to the people watching. They may not be able to name what they're responding to, but they feel it. The alignment between your message and your physical state creates a kind of trust that no amount of polished delivery can replicate.

The reverse is true as well. When you're nervous or self-conscious, your body contracts. Your breathing becomes shallow. Your gestures stiffen. Your voice tightens and loses its natural range. You shrink, and the person watching senses it, even through a screen.

This isn't something you need to fix with technique. It's something you need to notice. Most of the time, the physical signs of performance mode are already familiar to you. You know what it feels like when your shoulders creep up toward your ears, when your jaw tightens, when your breathing moves into your upper chest. The shift from performance to presence often starts with simply recognising that contraction and choosing to soften it.

A deep breath. A deliberate release of your shoulders. The feeling of your feet on the floor. These aren't tricks. They're ways of reminding your body of something it already knows how to do: be present.

Your voice follows the same pattern. When you're at ease, your voice finds its natural pitch, its natural rhythm, its natural warmth. When you're performing, it flattens out, speeds up, or tightens. The same awareness that helps you notice physical tension can help you notice vocal tension. And the same remedy applies: reconnect with your breath, slow down, and let your voice respond to what you're actually feeling rather than what you think you should sound like.

You don't need a perfect voice. You need a present one.

The Intention Effect

Presence isn't only physical. It's also about the quality of attention you bring to your communication.

There's a tangible difference between going through the motions and being fully engaged with what you're saying. Your audience can feel it. When you're connected to why your message matters, that conviction comes through in ways that have nothing to do with technique. Your eyes are more alive. Your words carry more weight. You're not reciting; you're sharing.

Before you hit record, it's worth taking a moment to reconnect with your intention. Not an intention about how you want to appear, but about what you want to offer. Ask yourself: why does this message matter to me? Who needs to hear it? What do I hope it does for the person watching?

These aren't rhetorical questions. They're a genuine reorientation. When your attention shifts from "How am I coming across?" to "How can I help the person watching this?", your energy shifts with it. The self-consciousness that fuels performance mode has nowhere to land when your focus is on service rather than approval.

This is what the best communicators do, whether they realise it or not. They're not thinking about their delivery. They're thinking about their audience. And that focus creates the very presence and authority that performance tries to manufacture but never quite achieves.

Returning to Presence

Presence isn't a state you achieve and hold permanently. It's something you drift away from and return to, again and again. Even people who are deeply comfortable on camera lose presence sometimes. They get distracted, self-conscious, or caught up in trying to get a point exactly right. The difference isn't that they never drift. It's that they notice when they have and they come back.

This is worth saying plainly, because the temptation is to treat presence as another form of perfection. Another standard to fall short of. But presence doesn't work that way. It's forgiving. It doesn't require you to be "on" every second. It only asks that when you notice you've left, you gently return.

In practice, this often looks quite simple. You're recording, and you catch yourself monitoring your own performance. You notice the familiar tightening. So you take a breath. You feel your feet on the floor. You remember who you're speaking to. And you continue.

Sometimes the return to presence happens mid-sentence. Sometimes you need to pause, regroup, and start the thought again. Both are fine. In fact, those moments of honest recovery often create more connection than unbroken fluency ever could. When you say "let me come back to that" or simply pause to collect your thoughts, your audience doesn't lose trust. They gain it, because they're watching someone who is genuinely present rather than performing.

This is the real skill of presence: not maintaining it perfectly, but returning to it willingly. And like any skill, it gets easier with practice. The gap between drifting and returning gets shorter. The recovery gets gentler. And eventually, presence becomes less something you do and more something you are.

Reality Check: Presence Isn't Complicated

*MYTH #1: "Presence is something
you either have or don't."*

Presence is a capacity, not a trait. Some people access it more easily than others, but everyone can develop it. Like any skill, it grows with attention and practice. The idea that you're either a "natural" or you're not is just another version of the fixed-confidence myth from the last chapter, wearing different clothes.

MYTH #2: "Being present means being unprepared."

Quite the opposite. Solid preparation is often what frees you to be present. When you know your material well enough that you don't need to cling to a script, you're free to respond to the moment, to adjust, to speak naturally. Preparation and presence aren't in tension. The first enables the second.

*MYTH #3: "You need to be
extroverted to have strong presence."*

Some of the most compelling communicators I've worked with are self-described introverts. Their thoughtfulness, their capacity for listening and their natural authenticity create a presence that's different from extroverted energy but no less powerful. Presence isn't about volume. It's about genuine connection.

MYTH #4: "Presence means maintaining
intense eye contact with the camera."

In real conversation, eye contact is dynamic. You look, you glance away, you look back. The same applies on camera. Staring unblinkingly at the lens doesn't create connection. It creates intensity. Letting your gaze be natural, the way it would be if you were talking to a friend, is far more engaging.

MYTH #5: "You need to be high-
energy to have good presence."

Authentic energy matters more than high energy. Different messages call for different tones, and forcing excitement when your message calls for something quieter undermines your credibility. The goal isn't to perform energy. It's to embody whatever energy is genuine for you and for what you're saying.

The Shift: When the Script Disappeared

A client I'll call James was preparing to pitch to a group of potential investors over a live video call. He'd done what most people do with high-stakes presentations: built a detailed slide deck that doubled as his script. Every point he wanted to make was tied to a slide. Every slide told him what to say next. The presentation wasn't just supporting his pitch. It was his pitch.

On the day of the call, the slides weren't there. He'd prepared the deck on his desktop, but the version on his laptop hadn't synced properly. By the time he realised, the investors were already on the call. There was no time to fix it.

He had two choices: cancel or carry on without the thing he'd built his entire delivery around.

He carried on. He talked them through the opportunity from memory, not from a script but from genuine understanding of what he was offering and why it mattered. When they asked detailed questions, he shared a PDF document he'd sent them in advance and walked them through the specifics from there. But the core of the pitch was just him, speaking honestly about something he believed in.

What he noticed afterwards was that the conversation had been different from every previous version of that pitch. When he'd had the slides, he'd been presenting. Moving through a sequence, hitting his marks, delivering the lines he'd rehearsed. Without them, he'd been responding. He was reading the room, adjusting to what the investors actually seemed interested in, answering the questions they were really asking rather than the ones he'd anticipated. He was present in a way the slides had never allowed him to be.

The pitch went well. But more than that, it changed how he thought about preparation. The slides had felt like his safety net. It turned out they'd been the thing standing between him and the room.

Flip the Switch: Your Return to Presence

These exercises aren't about adding new skills. They're about reconnecting with the presence you already have when you're not trying to perform.

Exercise 1: Your Presence Inventory

Think about the moments in your everyday life when you're most naturally present. Conversations where you forget to be self-conscious, activities where time disappears, situations where you feel fully yourself. Write down three to five of these. Then look at what they have in common. Is it familiarity? Purpose? Connection with the people involved? A sense of safety? These patterns are your natural pathways to presence, and they can be brought into your recording space.

Exercise 2: The Three-Breath Reset

Before your next recording, try this. First breath: breathe in fully and notice what you're feeling in your body. Second breath: breathe out slowly and consciously release tension from your shoulders, jaw and face. Third breath: breathe naturally and bring your attention to the person you're about to speak to. This takes about fifteen seconds. It's not a performance ritual. It's a way of arriving in the moment before you begin.

Exercise 3: Set Your Intention

Before you hit record, finish this sentence: "The person watching this needs to hear..." Let your answer be specific. Not a polished mission statement, but a plain, honest description of what you're offering and why it matters. Write it down and read it to yourself before you begin. Notice how your energy shifts when your focus moves from how you'll come across to what you're here to give.

Exercise 4: The Presence Anchor

Choose a physical object to place near your camera. Something that reminds you of why your message matters, or who it's for. It could be a photo, a word, a small object with personal meaning. Make it part of your setup. When you notice yourself slipping into performance mode during a recording, glance at it. Let it bring you back to your intention. Over time, the object becomes a shortcut: a quiet signal to your body and your mind that it's safe to be present rather than perform.

You don't need to master presence. You just need to practise returning to it. And each time you do, the old story, the one that says you need to be perfect, polished and performing to be worth watching, loses a little more of its hold.

INTEGRATING PART TWO

From Clarity to Decision

In these chapters, you've moved from a performance based idea of confidence to something far more useful. You've seen that:

- Confidence is internal trust, not external performance
- Presence is physical, not just mental
- People connect with what's real, not what's polished

Before you move on, take a moment to reflect: where in your life do you already trust yourself, even when things aren't perfect? And if your goal on camera shifted from performance to presence, what's the first thing you'd do differently?

Carry this forward: confidence is not something you manufacture. It's what's left when you stop trying to protect yourself. And now it's time to put that into practice.

PART III

THE MOMENT IT BECOMES REAL

Understanding is important, but it isn't the finish line.

At some point, the switch flips in the real world, not in your head. It happens the first time you show up when you would normally avoid it. The first time you stop editing yourself mid sentence. The first time you let a moment be imperfect and keep going.

In this part, we'll focus on the moments that actually create change, the small decisions that build trust in yourself. Not big dramatic breakthroughs, but repeatable turning points. You'll learn how to interrupt the old pattern when it shows up, and how to stay present when your body is signalling nerves.

This is where confidence stops being an idea and becomes an experience.

7

THE CONFIDENCE SWITCH

Something has shifted.

You may not have noticed it happening. There was no single moment where the ground moved. But if you've been sitting with what these chapters have asked you to consider, the old story doesn't hold together the way it used to.

You know the camera isn't the problem. You've seen that. You know perfectionism isn't a high standard, it's what keeps you stuck. You know confidence isn't a feeling you need to generate before you press record. It's what you already have when you stop trying to manufacture it.

None of that is news to you any more. So this chapter doesn't ask you to learn anything new. It asks you to notice what's already changed.

What You Already Know

Think about where you were when you opened this book. There was probably a version of confidence you believed in, one that looked polished and sounded certain and never stumbled. A version you'd been measuring yourself against and coming up short.

That version was never real. It was a performance standard dressed up as a personality trait. And by now, you know that.

You know that what looks like effortless confidence on screen is usually someone who has simply stopped monitoring themselves long enough to be present. You know that the people whose content moves you aren't flawless, they're honest. You know that the fear of being seen doesn't mean you're not ready. It means you're human.

You also know, if you're honest, that none of the things you thought you needed before you could show up were ever really necessary. Not the perfect lighting. Not the ideal script. Not the right mood or the right energy or the right version of yourself. Those were conditions you set, unconsciously, to keep the moment of actually doing it safely in the future.

And here is what changes when you see that clearly: the future stops being where your confidence lives. It stops being "I'll do it when." It becomes "I could do it now."

That shift, that quiet collapse of all the reasons to wait, is the confidence switch. Not a technique. Not a strategy. A recognition that you've been carrying something you don't need any more.

When It Becomes Real

This is the part that's difficult to describe, because it doesn't happen the way you'd expect.

You might imagine the switch as something dramatic. A moment of clarity that strikes like lightning and permanently rewires how you feel. But for most people, myself included, it's quieter than that. It feels less like a breakthrough and more like putting something down. A weight you'd been carrying for so long you'd stopped noticing it was there.

You already know my version. The day I stopped retaking and simply pressed record. One take. Imperfect. Real. What I haven't said is what it actually felt like in the moment, because it wasn't heroic. It was a softening. A small, private decision that the performance I'd been running was costing me more than it was worth. I didn't suddenly feel confident. I just stopped requiring myself to feel confident before I began.

That distinction matters. The switch isn't a surge of belief in yourself. It's the moment you stop making belief a prerequisite for action. It's the moment "I'm not ready" changes from a stop sign to a description of how you feel, which turns out to be irrelevant to whether you can begin.

And here is what makes this chapter different from everything that came before it. Parts One and Two showed you what was in the way. They dismantled the myths, named the patterns, redefined what confidence actually means. All of that was necessary. But understanding alone doesn't change anything. At some point, the understanding has to become a choice.

Not a dramatic, once-and-for-all choice. A quiet one. The choice to stop waiting for the feeling and start with the action. To stop performing and start being present. To trust that what you have to say matters more than how you look saying it.

That's the switch. And if you've been reading honestly, it may already be happening.

The Version of You That Already Knows

Here is what I want you to sit with for a moment. You've done this before.

Not on camera, perhaps. But you've had moments where you were fully present, fully yourself, and completely unselfconscious about it. Conversations where you forgot to monitor how you sounded. Moments where you helped someone and didn't think twice about whether you were doing it "right." Times when you spoke up because something needed saying, and it never occurred to you to rehearse it first.

That version of you, the one that shows up naturally when the stakes feel low and the connection feels real, isn't a different person. It's you without the performance layer. And everything you've read in this book has been building toward one simple recognition: the performance layer was never necessary. It was never what made you effective, or credible, or worth listening to. It was something you learned to put on because you believed the camera demanded it.

It doesn't. The camera is just a lens. The person on the other side is just a person. And you already know how to talk to people.

The switch isn't about becoming someone new. It's about stopping the effort of being someone you're not. It's about allowing the version of you that already knows how to do this, the one that's been there in every honest conversation and every unguarded moment, to be the version that shows up on camera too.

That might not sound like much. But for most people, it changes everything. Because the moment you stop trying to be confident is the moment confidence stops being something you chase and starts being something you recognise. It was always there. You just had to stop performing long enough to feel it.

Reality Check: The Switch Isn't Magical

MYTH #1: "One day it'll just happen."

That's the trap. Confidence doesn't arrive like a package you've been waiting for. It emerges when you decide to act, not when conditions finally feel perfect. The people who look confident on camera didn't wait for the feeling to show up first. They started before it did, and the feeling followed.

MYTH #2: "I need more
training before I can do this."

There's a difference between learning to grow and learning to delay. Preparation has real value, but at some point it stops being preparation and starts being a way to avoid the thing you're preparing for. If you're honest with yourself, you probably already know enough. The rest comes from doing.

MYTH #3: "I'll do it once I feel less afraid."

The feeling rarely comes first. Action changes how you feel, not the other way around. You don't wait out the fear and then begin. You begin, and the fear begins to lose its authority. That order never reverses, no matter how long you wait.

MYTH #4: "It won't work for me."

You already have the evidence. Think about moments when you've spoken up despite nerves, helped someone without rehearsing what to say, or shared something real because the person in front of you needed to hear it. Those weren't anomalies. They were your natural confidence working exactly as it always has. The switch is simply letting that version of you show up on camera too.

MYTH #5: *"The switch is all-or-nothing."*

It was never meant to be. The switch isn't a permanent state you achieve once and never lose. It's a choice you make each time you show up. Some days it will feel effortless. Other days you'll have to choose it deliberately. Both count. What matters isn't whether doubt shows up, it's whether doubt gets to decide what you do next.

The Shift: The Moment
I Stopped Waiting

I'd been trying to record a course for months. Not thinking about recording it. Actually trying. Sitting down, pressing record, getting a few minutes in, stopping, starting again. The material was solid. I knew it well. I was creating it with partners who were waiting on me to deliver it, and the longer it took, the more the pressure built.

That pressure made everything worse. Every time I sat down to record, the stakes felt higher than the last time. It wasn't just about getting it right any more. It was about justifying why it had taken so long. Each failed attempt raised the bar for what the next attempt needed to be, which made the next attempt even harder to start.

I tried everything I could think of. Better outlines. Tighter scripts. Different setups. More preparation. Less preparation. None of it worked, because the problem was never the preparation. The problem was that I was waiting to feel ready, and the feeling of readiness wasn't coming. If anything, it was getting further away.

The breaking point wasn't dramatic. It was quiet. I sat down one morning and said to myself, with something closer to exhaustion than courage: this way of working is never going to produce anything I'm happy with. There has to be another way.

So I tried something I hadn't tried before. I stopped trying to get it right. I hit record once, spoke the way I would if I were explaining the material to someone sitting across from me, and whatever came out in that take was the video. No retakes. No edits. One take.

It was imperfect. I knew that before I watched it back. But it was also real, and it was done. And when I saw the response, when my partners told me it was the most natural and engaging version of me they'd experienced, I realised something that changed how I worked from that point on.

The thing I'd been chasing through all those months of retakes had never been at the end of perfection. It had been available the whole time. I just had to stop performing long enough to let it through.

Flip the Switch: What's Your Moment of Decision?

You don't need a dramatic breakthrough. You just need a moment of decision.

Exercise 1: The Waiting Inventory

Ask yourself: what have I been waiting for?

Be specific. Is it a feeling? A circumstance? A level of preparation? Write down exactly what you've been telling yourself needs to happen before you can show up on camera. Then look at what you've written and ask one honest question: is this a genuine requirement, or is it a condition I've set to keep the moment safely in the future?

Exercise 2: The Honest Question

Think about the last time you talked yourself out of creating something. What reason did you give yourself? Write it down.

Now ask: if a friend told you this was the reason they hadn't started, what would you say to them? Write that down too. Notice the gap between what you accept from yourself and what you'd accept from someone you care about.

Exercise 3: The Smallest Step

What is the smallest action you could take today that would represent the switch in your life?

Not the ideal action. Not the one you'd take if you were braver or better prepared. The smallest one. Perhaps it's recording sixty seconds just for yourself. Perhaps it's committing to a single unscripted take. Write it down in specific terms: what you'll do, when you'll do it, and what "done" looks like.

Exercise 4: The Permission Statement

Complete this sentence: "Today, I give myself permission to..."

Make it specific to whatever has been holding you still. Don't overthink it. The first honest answer is usually the right one.

Exercise 5: Make It Real

Create a simple physical action that marks your decision. It might be placing a note by your camera, renaming your recording folder from "Drafts" to "Real Conversations," or setting a recurring appointment in your calendar called "Showing Up."

Then do it. Write it, say it aloud, and hit record.

And now the bridge is the only thing that needs to happen on camera, the question becomes: who are you actually talking to? Because the moment you stop speaking to an imaginary audience and start speaking to one real person, everything about how you communicate changes.

8

SPEAKING TO ONE PERSON

There's a question that changes everything about how you show up on camera. It isn't about lighting or scripts or delivery techniques. It's simpler than that, and more powerful.

Who are you talking to?

Not your audience. Not your followers. Not the algorithm. Who is the actual person on the other side of that lens, and what do they need to hear from you right now?

Most people never ask this question. They press record and speak to a crowd that isn't there, an imagined room full of strangers evaluating their performance. And that's exactly why it feels so unnatural. You're not wired to speak to a crowd. You're wired to speak to a person. The moment you make that shift, everything about your delivery, your energy and your confidence changes.

The Intimacy Advantage

Here's something I tell clients when they're nervous on camera: don't imagine a crowd. Don't imagine strangers. Imagine a friend. Someone who knows you. Someone who wants you to succeed. Someone who would genuinely benefit from what you're about to share. Then speak to them.

This isn't a trick. It's a return to how communication actually works.

When you speak to one person, the performance drops away almost immediately. Your tone warms up because you're no longer projecting to a room, you're talking to someone you care about. Your language gets more direct because jargon and abstraction feel wrong when you're speaking to a real human being. Your pacing becomes natural because you're not performing a script, you're having a conversation. Even your body changes. Your gestures get smaller and more genuine. Your face becomes more expressive. You stop monitoring yourself and start connecting.

And something happens to your conviction too. When you can picture the specific person your message is for, when you can imagine the difference it might make for them, you stop just sharing information and start helping someone. That shift from broadcasting to serving is one of the most powerful things you can do on camera. It doesn't just make your content better. It makes you feel different creating it.

If you don't have a specific person in mind, make one up. Picture your ideal client, or someone who asked you a thoughtful question recently. Anchor yourself in that connection. Because connection is what people respond to, not perfection.

The Power of Specificity

Here is the thing that feels counterintuitive until you see it in action: the more specific you make your audience, the more universal your impact becomes.

When you try to create content for everyone, you end up connecting deeply with no one. Your message becomes generic, your examples too broad, your language too careful. But when you create for someone specific, your content gains an honesty and relevance that resonates far beyond that one person.

Think about the content that has impacted you most. Chances are, it felt like it was made just for you. Like the creator somehow knew what you were thinking, what you were struggling with, what you needed to hear. That feeling wasn't an accident. It was the result of someone speaking to a specific person with a specific need, and in doing so, reaching everyone who shared it.

This is especially true for creators, coaches, educators and entrepreneurs. Your audience isn't tuning in for a polished performance. They're looking for someone who understands their situation and can help. When you speak to one person's real challenges, as if you were sitting across from them, your content stops being informational and starts being transformative. People don't want to be talked at. They want to be spoken to. And when you speak to one, you end up reaching many.

The Letter, Not the Speech

There's a simple test for whether your content is connecting or broadcasting. Ask yourself: does this sound like a speech, or does it sound like a letter to someone I care about?

Here's the difference.

The speech sounds like this: "Today I'd like to address the importance of proper nutrition for optimal health. Many studies have shown that a balanced diet containing adequate protein, complex carbohydrates and essential fatty acids can significantly impact overall wellness. In this video, we'll explore several nutritional principles that audience members can apply to their daily routines."

The letter sounds like this: "Hey Sarah, I've been thinking about our conversation last week when you mentioned feeling constantly tired despite getting enough sleep. I'm wondering if your nutrition might be playing a role. I've found a few simple changes that made a huge difference for me, and I thought they might help you too."

The content might cover the same ground. But the first creates distance. It positions you as separate from the person watching, delivering information from above. The second creates connection. It positions you alongside them, as someone who understands their situation and wants to help.

That difference isn't just about style. It changes how you feel while creating. The speech requires you to perform. The letter lets you be yourself. One triggers anxiety. The other feels natural.

So make it your practice. Don't write a script for a crowd. Write a letter to a friend. Don't perform a speech. Have a conversation. Don't try to sound like an expert. Try to sound like someone who cares. That shift in intention will transform how you feel, and how you're received.

Reality Check: You Aren't Speaking to a Crowd

MYTH #1: "I need to sound like a presenter."

The opposite is true. The most effective communicators on camera speak the way they'd speak to a colleague or a friend. Warmth and humanity will always land harder than polish and pitch. The moment you stop trying to sound like a presenter and start sounding like yourself, your audience leans in rather than tuning out.

MYTH #2: "I have to keep the energy high the whole time."

Grounded energy always lands harder than forced energy. In real conversation, you naturally vary your tone, pace and intensity based on what you're saying. That dynamic quality is what makes communication engaging. Forcing high energy throughout a video feels exhausting for you and unnatural for the person watching. Let your energy follow the message, not the other way around.

MYTH #3: "Speaking to one person feels too casual."

That's a feature, not a flaw. Casual creates comfort, and comfort creates trust. Professional doesn't mean formal. It means providing value with integrity. Some of the most respected voices in any field are the ones who make complex ideas feel accessible through conversational, relatable communication.

MYTH #4: "I need to cover everything for everyone."

Specificity is what makes content feel relevant. When you try to speak to everyone, your message becomes so broad it connects deeply with no one. Content that solves a specific problem for a specific person will always outperform generic content aimed at a wide audience. It will still help many people, but it helps them precisely because it feels like it was made for their situation.

MYTH #5: "Personal connection doesn't scale."

Every piece of content that's ever moved you felt personal. The most successful creators build audiences of thousands precisely because their content feels like a one-to-one conversation. If you create something that feels like a personal message to one ideal viewer, and a thousand people who fit that profile watch it, you've created a thousand personal connections through a single piece of content. Intimacy is what enables scale, not what prevents it.

The Shift: The Course That Started with One Person

This book grew out of a seven-video mini-course called The Confidence Switch. I recorded the whole thing in one afternoon, in one take per video. No scripts, no retakes. And the reason it came together that easily is the reason this chapter exists.

It started with a conversation. A member of the Digital Stage Academy, an expert in his field, told me he was struggling with impostor syndrome. He had the knowledge, the experience and the credibility, but he couldn't bring himself to create content. He felt like other people were doing it better, that he wasn't ready, that he didn't have anything worth saying. I'd heard versions of this before, but something about the way he described it stayed with me.

So when I sat down to record the course, I wasn't thinking about an audience. I wasn't thinking about reach or engagement or how the videos would perform. I was speaking to him. One person, with a real problem, who I genuinely wanted to help. That focus changed everything about how I delivered the material. I wasn't presenting. I was talking to someone I knew, about something that mattered to both of us.

Thousands of people have taken that course since. But the message that stopped me came recently, from someone who had watched all seven videos back to back. She wrote to tell me that the reframe of speaking to one person had completely transformed her thinking. She'd been procrastinating over her own course for months. After watching the videos, she turned on her camera and recorded the entire thing in an afternoon. One take per module. It was ready for launch.

The process I'd used to make the course had inspired her to use the very same process to make her own.

That's what happens when you speak to one person. You don't lose the audience. You find them, one at a time.

Flip the Switch: Who Are You Speaking To?

These exercises help you move from the idea of speaking to one person to actually doing it.

Exercise 1: Identify Your One Person

Write down the name of someone who could benefit from your message. A client, a friend, a colleague, someone who recently asked you a question you could answer well. If no specific individual comes to mind, try a different route: think about the version of yourself before you knew what you know now. What did that person need to hear? What were they struggling with? What would have made a difference?

If you're building for an audience you haven't met yet, create a composite. Give them a name, a background, a specific challenge. Make them real enough that you could imagine their reaction as you speak. The more specific the person, the more grounded your content will be.

Exercise 2: Core Transformations

For the person you identified in Exercise 1, complete these three sentences:

"If I could help them feel just one thing, it would be..." This is the emotional core of your message, the shift you're offering, not just the information.

"If I could help them understand just one thing, it would be..." This is the insight that would make the biggest difference for them right now.

"If I could inspire them to do just one thing, it would be..." This is the action you're hoping to set in motion.

Exercise 3: The Virtual Coffee

Imagine sitting across from your one person at a coffee shop. What would you say first? How would you describe your solution to them? What examples would you reach for? What questions might they ask? Write a brief outline of this imaginary conversation. Don't overthink it. Write the way you'd actually talk.

Exercise 4: Visual Anchor

Find or create a visual reminder of your one person. A photo, a name on a sticky note, even a single word that brings them to mind. Place it near your camera during your next recording session. This sounds small, but it works. When your eyes drift to that anchor mid-sentence, it pulls you back into connection and out of performance.

Exercise 5: Make It Real

Choose your next piece of content. Before you record it, spend sixty seconds with your one person in mind. Picture their face. Think about what they're dealing with. Then press record and talk to them.

Try this for your next three videos or content pieces. Notice how it changes both how you feel during creation and how your audience responds. The difference isn't just in your comfort level. It's in the connection you create.

And now there's one more thing to address. Because speaking to one person will change how your content feels immediately. But the question that follows is: what happens when you do it again? And again. And again. That's where confidence stops being a decision you make once and starts becoming something you carry with you.

9

THE POWER OF PRACTICE, NOT PERFECTION

You've made the decision. You know who you're speaking to. Now there's one question left: what happens when you do it again tomorrow? And the day after that? And the week after that?

Because the confidence switch doesn't stay on by itself. It stays on through practice. Not perfect practice. Not dramatic, high-stakes practice. Just the quiet, consistent habit of showing up and doing the thing, even when it doesn't feel particularly brave or inspired or ready.

That's where confidence actually lives. Not in the single breakthrough moment, but in what you do with the days that follow it.

The Rhythm of Showing Up

Think about going to the gym. The first few sessions feel awkward. You're not sure you're doing it right. You're convinced everyone is watching. You leave wondering whether it's even working. But you go back. And somewhere around the third or fourth week, something shifts. You stop thinking about how it looks and start noticing how it feels. The awkwardness fades, not because you've mastered anything, but because the unfamiliarity has worn off.

The same thing happens with content creation.

When I started using a one-take workflow, it wasn't because I was fearless. It was because I was tired of letting fear run the process. So I committed to showing up repeatedly, even when I didn't feel ready. And with every take, something changed. Not my skill level, at least not at first. What changed was my relationship with the discomfort. It stopped being a wall and started being weather. Something I moved through rather than something that stopped me.

That's what consistent practice does. It doesn't make the nerves disappear. It changes what the nerves mean. The first time you press record feeling uncertain, it feels like evidence that you shouldn't be doing this. The tenth time, it just feels like how it starts. The fiftieth time, you barely notice it. Not because the feeling has gone, but because you've stopped treating it as a reason to stop.

And something else happens that most people don't expect. Each time you show up, you're sending yourself a quiet message: "I can do this, even when it's uncomfortable." Over time, that message shifts. It goes from "I'm not sure I can" to "I've done this before" to "this is just what I do." That progression is the growth of genuine confidence, and it only happens through repetition. Not through one perfect video. Not through waiting until you feel ready. Through the rhythm of doing it again and again, and letting the doing teach you what no amount of preparation ever could.

This is also why I encourage creators to build habits around content rather than treating each piece as a high-stakes event. Confidence doesn't live in the big launch or the viral moment. It lives in the Tuesday afternoon when nobody is watching and you press record anyway. It grows through the doing.

The Messy Middle

There's a stretch in every creative practice where the results don't match the effort. You're showing up consistently, but the videos still feel awkward. You're doing the work, but the growth isn't visible yet. You cringe at your own recordings. You compare your early attempts to someone else's polished high-light reel and wonder whether you're cut out for this.

This is what I call the messy middle, and it's where most people quit.

It feels like failure, but it's actually the opposite. The discomfort you feel watching your earlier work is evidence that your standards are evolving faster than your output. That's a sign of growth, not a sign that you should stop. Every expert creator you admire has a folder of videos they never published, a stretch where they wondered if it was working, a phase where the gap between what they wanted to create and what they were actually producing felt unbridgeable.

The difference between those who develop lasting confidence and those who don't isn't talent. It's who stays in the game long enough to push through this phase.

What helps during the messy middle is shifting what you measure. Instead of judging individual pieces of content, pay attention to the process itself. Is it becoming more comfortable? Are you recovering from stumbles more quickly? Are you spending less time overthinking before you press record? Those are the metrics that matter, because they compound. Small, barely visible improvements that stack on top of each other until one day the thing that used to terrify you just feels like something you do.

The other thing that helps is recognising that skill development isn't linear. It follows a stair-step pattern: long plateaus where nothing seems to change, followed by sudden jumps in ability. The plateaus are exactly when most people quit, not realising that the jump might be days away. If you can learn to trust the process during those flat stretches, you'll outlast every person who needed visible progress to keep going.

The Relationship That Grows

Every time you speak on camera, you're building a relationship. With the lens, with your voice, with your story. And like any relationship, it deepens with time and attention.

At first, the camera feels like a stranger. Someone you're nervous around, someone you try to impress, someone whose judgment you're acutely aware of. But with enough consistent interaction, that changes. The stranger becomes familiar. The thing you were performing for becomes a tool you're working with. The lens stops feeling like a critic and starts feeling like a collaborator, something that helps you reach the people you're here to serve.

This evolution doesn't happen through occasional high-pressure appearances. It happens through the ordinary, unremarkable act of showing up regularly. Through treating content creation as a practice rather than a performance. Through pressing record on the days when you don't feel inspired, and discovering that those are often the days that matter most.

Many of my clients are surprised to find that with enough practice, they start to genuinely enjoy being on camera. What once triggered anxiety becomes a source of creative expression and connection. That shift isn't magic. It's the natural result of doing something often enough that it stops being an event and starts being a part of who you are.

Reality Check: Practice Isn't Failure

*MYTH #1: "If I'm still nervous, I
must be doing something wrong."*

Nerves aren't a sign that something is wrong. They're a sign that you care about what you're doing. Professional performers, experienced speakers and seasoned athletes still feel pre-performance anxiety after years of practice. The difference is they've stopped treating that feeling as a reason not to begin. The goal was never to eliminate nerves. It was to keep moving despite them.

*MYTH #2: "If I need practice,
I must not be very good."*

The best in any field never stop practising. Athletes don't stop training once they're skilled. Musicians don't stop rehearsing once they can play the piece. They practise because that's what mastery looks like. The people who are genuinely good at something are almost always the ones who show up most consistently, not the ones who needed the least preparation.

MYTH #3: "If it's not working, I should stop."

If it's not working yet, you're in the process, not at the end of it. Improvement is rarely visible from the inside while it's happening. You're often closer to a breakthrough than you think, especially during the stretches where it feels like nothing is changing. The only way this doesn't work is if you stop completely.

MYTH #4: "Once I've practised enough, I'll never feel insecure again."

Confidence was never meant to be a fixed state. There will always be new challenges, unfamiliar formats and moments where doubt shows up again. What practice gives you isn't immunity from insecurity. It gives you a foundation to return to, a track record that reminds you: I've felt this before, and I kept going, and it was fine.

MYTH #5: "Some people just have natural camera confidence."

What looks like natural talent almost always has years of repetition behind it. Nobody is born knowing how to connect through a lens. The people who seem instantly comfortable on camera have usually spent years developing related skills in other contexts: teaching, public speaking, storytelling, performing. And even those with transferable skills still had to adapt specifically to camera work through practice.

The Shift: The Practice That Never Finishes

I'd been coaching someone for several months who had been creating videos consistently. He'd adopted the one-take approach, showed up regularly, and kept publishing even when he wasn't happy with the results. By most measures, he was doing everything right.

But he didn't feel like he was doing everything right. He'd watch his videos back and see everything that was wrong with them. The phrasing that wasn't quite sharp enough. The moments where his energy dipped. The sections where he lost his thread for a second before finding it again. He kept going, but with a growing sense that the gap between where he was and where he wanted to be wasn't closing.

One day he told me, honestly, that he didn't think he'd ever be as good at this as I was. He admired what I did on camera and couldn't see himself reaching that level.

I told him something that surprised him. I feel exactly the same way about my own content. Every video I make, I can see what I'd do differently. Every time I watch something back, there's a moment I'd change, a phrase I'd sharpen, an idea I didn't land as well as I wanted to. I'm never fully satisfied. The difference is that I've made peace with that dissatisfaction. I'm happy being unhappy about it, because that restlessness is what makes me want to do it better next time.

He went quiet for a moment. Then he said something that told me he'd got it. That was exactly what was driving him too. He'd just been interpreting the dissatisfaction as failure rather than as fuel.

That's the thing about practice that most people miss. You don't reach a point where you think, "I've mastered this now." There's always something to improve, always something to make better. The goal was never perfection. The practice is the work. Not a phase you pass through on the way to getting it right, but the thing itself. And once he saw that, the pressure to arrive somewhere lifted, and what was left was just the rhythm of showing up and getting slightly better each time.

Flip the Switch: What's Your Next Step?

You don't need to practise perfectly. You just need to start, and then keep going.

Exercise 1: Your Practice Commitment

What specific practice could you commit to that feels challenging but doable? Not ambitious enough to abandon after a week. Not so small it doesn't stretch you. Something you could sustain even during a busy stretch.

It might be recording sixty seconds of unscripted video every day, just for yourself. It might be going live once a week to a small or private audience. It might be keeping a practice folder where you save recordings you never post, just to build the habit of pressing record without the pressure of publishing.

Whatever you choose, write it down in specific terms: what you'll do, how often, and for how long. "I will record one unscripted sixty-second video every weekday morning for the next four weeks." A commitment that specific is harder to negotiate your way out of than a vague intention to "create more content."

Exercise 2: The Readiness Reframe

Complete these three sentences:

"I've been waiting to feel ready before I..."

"If I stopped waiting for readiness, the first step I would take is..."

"One small action I could take today, exactly as I am, is..."

Don't edit yourself. Write the first honest answer that comes. The gap between what you've been waiting for and what you could do right now is usually much smaller than it feels.

Exercise 3: Progress Metrics

Think about how you currently judge whether your content is "working." If the answer involves likes, views, comments or shares, you're measuring the wrong thing, at least at this stage.

Choose two or three metrics that measure your practice rather than your audience's response. Things you have complete control over. Things that track whether you're showing up, not whether the world is applauding. Write them down and commit to tracking them for the duration of your practice commitment from Exercise 1.

Exercise 4: Your Messy Middle Plan

At some point during your practice commitment, you'll hit a stretch where it feels pointless. The improvement will stall, the motivation will dip, and the voice in your head will suggest that this isn't working and you should probably stop.

When that moment comes, what will you do? Write down one specific action you can take to keep going. It might be reaching out to a specific person for perspective. It might be revisiting your earliest recordings to see how far you've come. It might simply be lowering the bar for that day: record thirty seconds instead of sixty, but don't break the streak. Decide now, while your clarity is high, so you don't have to figure it out when your motivation is low.

Exercise 5: Make It Real

Whatever you wrote down in Exercise 1, do the first one today. Not tomorrow. Not when you feel ready. Today.

If the full commitment feels too much for right now, do the smallest possible version of it. Record fifteen seconds instead of sixty. Go live for two minutes instead of twenty. Open the camera app and press record and say one sentence. The size doesn't matter. What matters is that the practice starts today, not in some future moment when conditions feel right.

Something has changed by now, whether you've fully noticed it or not. The decision you made in Chapter 7 wasn't a theory. You've started to feel what it's like to speak to a real person instead of performing for an imaginary crowd. And if you've begun practising, even once, you've felt the difference between waiting for confidence and building it.

The switch isn't a single moment. It's something you've been doing, chapter by chapter, page by page. And the fact that it doesn't feel dramatic is exactly the point. The most lasting changes rarely do.

INTEGRATING PART THREE

From Decision to Practice

These three chapters weren't about learning something new. They were about recognising what's already changed.

- The confidence switch isn't earned through preparation. It's a decision you make when you stop requiring readiness as a prerequisite for action.
- Speaking to one person transforms both how you feel creating content and how that content is received.
- Practice doesn't make perfect. It makes familiar. And familiar is where confidence lives.

Take a moment to sit with this: who is the one person you could speak to the next time you press record, and what would it take to make that a habit rather than a one-off?

The foundation is built. What comes next is making it yours.

PART IV

THE POWER YOU'VE ALWAYS POSSESSED

By the time you reach this part, the goal isn't to "get confident".

It's to stop leaving yourself the moment the camera turns on.

In this final part, we'll bring it all together, not just for video, but for the way you show up in conversations, leadership and life. Confidence becomes less like something you chase, and more like something you inhabit. A steady, practical ability to stay connected, to speak clearly, and to let your message matter more than your image.

You won't need a new personality. You won't need a persona.

You'll simply be able to show up as you are, on purpose.

10

AUTHENTICITY IS MAGNETIC

Something happens when you stop performing and start showing up.

It's not dramatic. There's no single moment when everything clicks into place. But over time, as you practise presence instead of performance, as you speak to one person instead of broadcasting to a crowd, something shifts in what your audience receives. They stop watching your content and start feeling it. They stop evaluating you and start trusting you.

That shift has a name. It's authenticity. And it's the most powerful thing you can bring to a camera.

The Authenticity Advantage

Authenticity is alignment. It's what happens when who you are internally matches how you express yourself externally, when your message, your delivery and your intention all come from the same place. It's the absence of performance and the presence of truth.

In a landscape saturated with carefully curated content,

that kind of realness is rare. And because it's rare, it stands out. Not because it's polished or clever, but because it feels different. When someone is genuinely themselves on camera, you notice. The guard is down. The script is gone. What's left is a human being talking to another human being, and that creates a fundamentally different kind of connection.

This is why authenticity matters so much for creators, coaches, educators and entrepreneurs. Your audience isn't just buying your product, service or information. They're investing in a relationship with you. And relationships built on authenticity have a staying power that performance can never match.

That staying power comes down to trust. When you're willing to show up as yourself, imperfections included, you communicate something that no amount of polish can replicate: that you have nothing to hide. That transparency becomes the foundation of trust. It signals a groundedness that audiences instinctively respect. It creates consistency, because an authentic communicator doesn't present one version of themselves on camera and another off camera. And it opens the door to real connection, because when you share not just your expertise but your experience, your audience begins to see themselves in your story.

In a world where so much of what we consume feels manufactured, authenticity lands not as a strategy but as a relief.

Selective Transparency

One of the most common misconceptions about authenticity is that it requires revealing everything about yourself. It doesn't.

Authenticity isn't oversharing. It's genuine self-expression within appropriate boundaries. It's being real without being raw in ways that make your audience uncomfortable or pull focus from your message.

Think of it as selective transparency. You're choosing to

share aspects of yourself and your experience that serve your audience and support your message, while keeping appropriate privacy around areas that don't. A financial coach might share their past struggles with debt to connect with clients facing similar challenges. But they don't need to share the intimate details of their marriage or every personal purchase they make.

The question isn't "Am I sharing everything?" It's "Am I presenting a genuine version of myself that aligns with my values and serves my audience?"

This distinction matters because it removes one of the biggest barriers to authenticity: the fear that being real means being exposed. It doesn't. Authenticity gives you full permission to have boundaries. What it asks is that within those boundaries, you're honest. That the version of you the audience sees is a true version, not a manufactured one.

Your authentic voice isn't something you need to invent. It's already there, underneath the layers of "shoulds" and professional personas we tend to adopt, especially on camera. Most people already have it. They just haven't given themselves permission to use it in front of a lens.

The Courage to Be Imperfect

If authenticity is this simple, why does it feel so hard?

Because there are real forces working against it. Most of them are invisible, which makes them harder to name and harder to resist.

The first is the expert trap. Many professionals feel pressure to maintain a flawless "expert" image that leaves no room for humanity. The result is stiff, formal communication that creates distance instead of connection. The irony is that audiences trust the expert who occasionally says "I don't know" far more than the one who never admits uncertainty.

Then there's the comparison pull. Spending time watching

others in your field can be valuable, but it can also lead to mimicry rather than genuine expression. When you're trying to be a version of someone else, it always reads as slightly off. People can feel the gap between the voice you're borrowing and the one that's actually yours.

And underneath both of these sits something we've already explored in this book: perfectionism. When you're focused on getting everything right, you sacrifice the natural qualities that make your communication engaging. Perfectionism and authenticity pull in opposite directions. One demands control. The other requires release.

Perhaps the most subtle barrier is approval-seeking. When your primary goal is to please everyone, you inevitably water down your message, mute your personality and present a sanitised version of yourself that connects deeply with no one. Authenticity asks you to accept that not everyone will resonate with you, and to see that as a feature, not a flaw.

Recognising these patterns is useful. But the real shift is simpler than dismantling each one individually. It's giving yourself permission to be imperfect.

That permission doesn't require a dramatic act of vulnerability. It's the small, consistent choice to show up as yourself even when it would be easier to hide behind a script or a professional persona. It's allowing your natural warmth or humour or thoughtfulness to come through, rather than adopting what you think a "professional" should sound like. It's acknowledging when you don't have all the answers rather than pretending to a certainty you don't feel.

These choices might seem small. But each one reinforces the same thing: that you trust yourself enough to be seen as you actually are. And the more you make that choice, the easier it becomes. You no longer need to maintain a separate camera persona. You no longer need to memorise the "right" way to present yourself. You simply show up, present with your message and your audience. That simplicity is freeing. And that freedom is what your audience responds to.

Reality Check: Authenticity Isn't Risky

MYTH #1: "Authenticity means
being exactly the same in all contexts."

Authentic people still adapt to different situations. A teacher speaks differently in a classroom than at a dinner party, but can be genuine in both settings. Authenticity isn't rigid consistency across every context. It's honest alignment between who you are and how you express yourself in each one.

MYTH #2: "Being authentic means being unfiltered."

There's a difference between being genuine and having no boundaries. Just as you wouldn't share every thought in a face-to-face conversation, you don't need to share everything on camera to be authentic. Selective transparency that serves your audience is still authenticity. Boundaries don't make you less real. They make your authenticity sustainable.

MYTH #3: "If I'm authentic, everyone will like me."

Authenticity might actually narrow your appeal, and that's a good thing. When you show up as yourself, you connect more deeply with the people who resonate with who you actually are, while others may not connect at all. The result is a smaller but far more engaged and loyal audience. That trade-off is worth making every time.

MYTH #4: "Authenticity doesn't
work in my professional field."

Every field has space for authentic communication, though what it looks like will vary. In more traditional industries, authenticity might mean straightforward language instead of jargon, or acknowledging limitations rather than overpromising. The expression changes. The principle doesn't.

MYTH #5: "Being authentic
means never changing or growing."

Growth is one of the most authentic things a person can do. Your perspectives, your style and your approach will naturally develop over time. Authenticity isn't about remaining static. It's about honestly representing where you are in each moment, which includes the fact that you're still evolving.

The Shift: The Expert Who Disappeared

I once worked with a financial planner who was warm, sharp and genuinely engaging in person. The kind of person who made you feel at ease within minutes of meeting her. She had a natural warmth that drew people in, and in conversation she could make even the most complex financial concepts feel approachable.

Her content was a different story. On camera, she became someone else entirely. She called it her "financial planning expert" mode: measured, formal, careful. Every video was technically competent, well structured and thoroughly researched. It was also completely forgettable. Her audience wasn't growing, engagement was minimal, and the content wasn't landing the way she knew it should.

When I watched her videos alongside a real conversation with her, the gap was obvious. The person on camera wasn't her. I asked her about it directly. She was clear: people would potentially be trusting her with their finances. She couldn't afford to come across as anything less than completely professional. Warmth and personality felt like a risk she wasn't willing to take.

I asked a simple question. Wouldn't part of that trust come from the fact that someone is warm, caring and human? People don't just hand over their finances to competence. They hand them over to someone they feel genuinely connected to.

She was reluctant. But she tried it. She dropped the formal delivery, stopped scripting every line, and let her natural conversational style into the content.

The response was immediate. Existing followers told her they loved seeing this side of her. Comments increased. Average views climbed steadily and kept climbing. People who had been passively watching started engaging.

She never went back to the old style. And the thing she told me afterwards was perhaps the most telling part: it was so much easier to create this way, because she'd stopped putting on an act.

The expertise hadn't changed. The person delivering it had simply shown up.

Flip the Switch: Finding Your Authentic Voice

These exercises help you identify what your authentic voice actually sounds like, so you can bring more of it to your content.

Exercise 1: Your Authentic Conditions

Think about when you feel most naturally yourself. Write down three to five specific situations where you forget to monitor yourself and are fully natural. For each one, identify what conditions make that possible. Is it the people? The topic? The setting? Then consider: which of those conditions could you recreate when you're creating content?

Exercise 2: The Outside View

Ask someone who knows you well what they find distinctive about how you communicate. Not what you're good at in general, but what's specifically yours: your rhythm, your way of explaining things, your energy. Their answer will likely point to qualities you take for granted but that your audience would respond to.

Exercise 3: The Borrowed Voice Audit

Complete these sentences:

"The qualities that make me effective in person that I want to bring more fully to my content are..."

"The communication patterns I've adopted that don't feel like mine are..."

"My natural way of explaining concepts involves..."

This isn't about judging what you've borrowed from others.

It's about noticing which parts of your on-camera communication actually feel like you, and which ones you've taken on because you thought you should.

Exercise 4: The Authenticity Experiment

Create a short piece of content that deliberately breaks one "rule" you've been following that doesn't feel authentic to you. Maybe it's speaking more casually, using a personal story, showing more emotion or structuring things differently than you normally would. Create it just for yourself. No pressure to share it unless you choose to.

Exercise 5: Make It Real

Record a 60-second video explaining something you care about, as if you were talking to a close friend. No script. No second take. Watch it back and notice what feels like you. That's what your audience needs to see more of.

Once you've found that voice, the question becomes a practical one: how do you bring it with you into the specific situations where it matters most?

11

PRACTICAL APPLICATIONS

You already know what the confidence switch is. You've felt it: the shift from performing to being present, from broadcasting to speaking to one person, from chasing perfection to simply showing up. But there's a moment, somewhere between understanding the switch and living it, where a familiar question appears.

What about webinars, though? What about going live? What about sales videos?

It's a reasonable question. Different formats feel different. A 30-second Instagram reel has nothing in common with a 60-minute webinar, and neither one resembles a virtual team meeting or a course recording you know will be watched for years. Each one seems to demand its own version of confidence.

But here's what's actually happening. The switch doesn't change. The triggers do.

The Same Switch, Different Rooms

Every content format has its own version of the performance trap. On social media, it's the visible metrics: the likes, shares and comments that turn every post into a public scorecard. In longer presentations and webinars, it's the sustained duration, the formality, the pressure to maintain energy without the feedback loop of a live audience. In live streaming, it's the inability to edit, which hands the microphone directly to your inner perfectionist. In sales videos, it's the conversion pressure, which tempts you to adopt a persona you'd never use in a real conversation. In course creation, it's the permanence: the knowledge that this recording will represent you for months or years.

These triggers feel different from each other. But they're all doing the same thing. They're pulling you out of presence and into performance. They're activating the same patterns you've been unravelling throughout this book: the need to get it right, the fear of being judged, the belief that you need to be a different version of yourself to be effective.

Which means the response is the same too.

When social media metrics start driving your creative decisions, the answer isn't a social media strategy. It's the same shift you made in Chapter 5: from seeking approval to offering value. When a webinar feels overwhelming, the answer isn't a more detailed script. It's the same one-person focus from Chapter 8, applied section by section. When live streaming feels terrifying because you can't edit, the answer isn't a cleverer content framework. It's the same relationship with imperfection you developed in Chapter 4 and practised in Chapter 9.

One of my clients struggled with this exact pattern. She was comfortable recording short educational videos but froze whenever she tried to go live. She'd spent weeks researching live-streaming strategies, collecting tips and frameworks, convinced that live content required a completely different skill set. When we looked at what was actually happening, the issue wasn't the format. It was that the inability to edit activated her perfectionism in a way that pre-recorded videos didn't. Once she recognised the trigger, she didn't need a live-streaming strategy. She needed to apply the same presence practice she already had, in a room where the stakes felt higher. Within a few sessions, the format stopped being the problem. It had never been the problem.

The format is never the problem. It's the room you're standing in. The switch you flip is the same one, regardless of the room.

Removing the Friction

There's one practical area worth addressing directly, not because it changes the switch, but because it can make the switch harder to flip.

Your technical setup.

This isn't about production quality. The most impactful creators often started with phone cameras, natural window light and built-in microphones. Their impact came from presence, not from equipment. But there's a difference between a simple setup and a distracting one. When your camera angle makes you self-conscious, when your audio forces your audience to strain, when your background competes with your message or your chair makes you fidget, those are friction points. They pull you out of presence and into self-monitoring. And self-monitoring is the enemy of connection.

The goal isn't to look or sound professional. It's to remove the things that get in the way.

That means positioning your camera at roughly eye level, because a natural conversation angle lets you forget the camera is there. It means having enough light on your face that your expressions are visible, because expression is how human beings connect. It means audio that's clear enough that your audience doesn't have to work to hear you. A basic external microphone handles this. It means a background that doesn't compete for attention, a setup that lets your body be comfortable, and notifications turned off so nothing pulls you out of the moment.

None of these need to be perfect. All of them need to be good enough that you can stop thinking about them. That's the test. If a technical element supports your ability to be present, keep it. If it creates another layer of performance pressure, simplify until it becomes invisible.

The equipment doesn't create confidence. But it can remove one more reason to not feel it.

You Already Know What to Do

If you've been reading this chapter waiting for the format-specific strategy that will finally make you confident on camera, this is the part where I tell you it doesn't exist.

Not because the problem is unsolvable, but because you've already solved it.

You know that confidence is trust, not performance. You know that presence is about being with your audience, not impressing them. You know that speaking to one person changes everything about how you communicate. You know that practice isn't about getting it right but about building a relationship with showing up. You know that authenticity is what your audience actually responds to.

These aren't abstract ideas. You've sat with them, questioned them and, if the earlier chapters did their job, begun to feel the truth in them. The switch isn't something you need to learn differently for each format. It's something you carry with you.

The temptation at this point is to keep collecting strategies.

To find one more framework, one more technique, one more system that will make the next format feel safe before you try it. That instinct is understandable. It's also the old pattern in disguise. It's the belief that you're not ready yet, dressed up as preparation.

You're ready. The switch works in every room. The only thing left is to walk in and flip it.

Reality Check: The Format Isn't the Problem

MYTH #1: "Each content format requires a completely different confidence strategy."

The triggers change but the switch doesn't. Social media, webinars, live streams and sales videos all activate different versions of the same performance trap. The principles that work in one format, presence, connection, speaking to one person, work in all of them. What changes is the surface. What stays the same is everything that matters.

MYTH #2: "I need professional equipment before I can create confident content."

Some of the most trusted voices online started with a phone and a window. Equipment can remove friction, but it doesn't create confidence. If upgrading your setup makes you more comfortable, it's worth doing. If it becomes another reason to delay, it's the old perfectionism wearing a new costume.

MYTH #3: "Live formats are harder than recorded ones."

They're different, not harder. Live content removes the option to edit, which can feel exposing. But it also removes the trap of endless retakes, which is where most performance anxiety actually lives. Many creators find that once they get past the first few minutes, live formats are easier because there's no temptation to start over.

*MYTH #4: "I should feel confident
in one format before I try another."*

Confidence doesn't transfer automatically, but the switch does. Waiting until you feel completely comfortable in one format before moving to the next is another version of waiting until you're ready. You'll build confidence in each format by practising in it, not by mastering a different one first.

*MYTH #5: "Following best practices
will make me more confident."*

Best practices can give you a starting structure, but they can also pull you away from authenticity. If a strategy doesn't feel like you, it won't serve you, regardless of how well it works for someone else. The most effective approach in any format is the one that lets you be present and genuine. That's not a best practice. That's your practice.

The Shift: The Same Switch, Live

A client I'll call Rachel had become genuinely comfortable on camera. I'd coached her through the one-take production method, and she'd taken to it. She could sit down, press record, deliver her material clearly and naturally, switch between scenes, and publish without needing a single retake. The performance trap that had held her back for months was behind her.

Then she decided she wanted to try live streaming. And everything she'd learned seemed to vanish overnight.

It made no sense on paper. She already recorded in one take. She already published without editing. The live stream would be, mechanically, almost identical to what she was doing every week. But something about the word "live" changed the equation entirely. The safety net she'd never actually used suddenly felt essential now that it was officially gone.

When we talked it through, the fear wasn't about capability. It was about the idea of live. She'd built her confidence around a process that technically allowed her to start over, even though she never did. The moment that option was formally removed, the old performance anxiety found a new door to walk through.

I pointed out what she already knew but hadn't quite connected: she did this already. Every video she published was effectively a live take. The only difference was that this time, people would be watching in real time. And that wasn't a threat. It was actually an advantage.

She tried it. And what she discovered surprised her. The live audience didn't make it harder. It made it easier. She could see names appearing, faces in their profile photos, comments coming in. The feedback she'd never had while recording alone was suddenly there, and it pulled her further into connection rather than performance.

The format hadn't required new confidence. It had asked her to trust the confidence she'd already built. The switch she'd learned to flip in one room worked in every room. She just had to walk in and find out.

Flip the Switch: The Confidence Switch in Practice

The switch doesn't change when the format does. These exercises help you prove that to yourself.

Exercise 1: Name Your Trigger

Choose the content format that feels most challenging to you right now. Write down exactly what makes it feel harder than other formats. Is it the visible metrics? The permanence? The inability to edit? The conversion pressure? Once you've named the specific trigger, ask yourself: which of the patterns from earlier in this book is this trigger activating? Perfectionism? Approval-seeking? The belief that you're not ready? Naming the trigger is how you stop the format from feeling like the problem.

Exercise 2: The One-Person Reset

Before your next piece of content, regardless of format, take ten seconds to picture one specific person who needs what you're about to share. Not an audience. Not a demographic. One person with a real question or a real problem that your content addresses. Let that person be the reason you hit record or go live. Notice how your energy shifts when you're speaking to them instead of performing for everyone.

Exercise 3: The Conversation Test

After you've recorded or delivered any piece of content, ask yourself one question: "Would I have said it that way to someone I care about?" If the answer is no, identify what changed. Where did you shift from connection to performance? This isn't about judgment. It's about awareness. The gap between how you speak to someone you trust and how you speak on camera is the gap the switch is designed to close.

Exercise 4: The Friction Audit

Look at your current recording or presenting setup. For each element (camera position, lighting, audio, background, physical comfort, notes, notifications), ask one question: does this support my ability to be present, or does it create pressure? Anything that creates pressure, simplify or remove. Anything that supports presence, keep. The goal is a setup you can forget about once you start.

Exercise 5: Make It Real

Choose a format you've been avoiding. Record one piece of content in that format, applying only the principles you already know: presence, one person, authenticity. No new strategies. No research beforehand. Just the switch. Watch it back and notice what worked.

And as you do, something starts to happen. The switch stops being something you flip deliberately and starts becoming the way you show up.

12

THE CONFIDENCE LOOP

By now, you've done something that matters, whether you realise it or not.

Maybe you've already been putting this into practice. You've sat in front of a camera, chosen presence over performance and pressed record knowing it wouldn't be flawless. Or maybe you haven't recorded anything yet. Maybe you've simply been reading, and somewhere along the way the old beliefs started losing their grip. The idea that you need to be perfect before you can be visible. The fear that the camera will expose something you'd rather hide. The story that confidence is something other people have and you don't.

Either way, something has moved. Whether you've been doing the work or simply confronting the thinking that's kept you from starting, you're not standing in the same place you were at the beginning of this book.

What happens next is worth understanding, because it's not just progress. It's the beginning of a pattern that sustains itself.

Something has already started to change.

You may not have named it yet. But if you've been sitting with the ideas in this book, if you've begun to practise even a few of them, you've probably noticed moments where the old weight isn't there. Moments where you sat down to record and the dread didn't show up. Moments where you spoke to the camera and forgot, even briefly, that it was there at all.

Those moments aren't accidents. They're the beginning of something.

Building Momentum

Here's what happens when you show up with presence instead of performance. You connect. Your audience feels it. You feel it too. And because it felt real, because it wasn't exhausting the way performing always was, you're more willing to do it again. So you do. And it's a little easier the second time. A little more natural the third. Each time you choose presence, the next choice becomes lighter.

This is the confidence loop. It's not a technique. It's not something you have to manage or optimise. It's what naturally happens when you stop performing and start showing up consistently.

The key word is consistently. Not perfectly. Not frequently. Consistently. The creator who records one honest video every week builds more lasting confidence than the one who produces a burst of polished content and then disappears for a month. It's not the quality of any single piece that strengthens the loop. It's the act of returning.

This is why confidence doesn't come from one break-through moment, no matter how powerful that moment feels. It comes from the rhythm of showing up, again and again, until the showing up itself becomes familiar. Until your body stops bracing for the thing it used to fear. Until the camera becomes what it was always meant to be: a way of connecting with someone who needs what you have to say.

Over time, the loop accelerates quietly. What once required

a conscious decision starts to happen on its own. The switch, which you used to flip deliberately before each recording, begins to stay on. Your default shifts. Not from anxiety to perfection, but from anxiety to presence.

That doesn't mean the doubt disappears entirely. It means the doubt stops being in charge. It becomes background noise rather than the thing running the show. You'll still have days when it's louder. Days when the old stories try to reassert themselves. But the loop is stronger than any single bad day, because it's built on repetition, not on feeling.

And here's what makes the loop different from discipline or willpower: it doesn't require you to push through. It carries you. Each time you show up and experience even a small moment of genuine connection, the loop does the work of making the next time easier. You're not forcing yourself forward. You're being drawn forward by something that already feels true.

The Art of Coming Back

The loop will break. Not if. When.

You'll get harsh feedback that lands harder than you expected. You'll have a technical failure in the middle of something important. You'll watch someone else's content and feel that familiar pull of comparison. You'll go through a period where life gets in the way and you stop creating for a while. And when you come back, the old resistance will be waiting, as if you never left.

This is normal. It doesn't mean the loop has failed. It means you're human.

The difference between someone who builds lasting confidence and someone who doesn't isn't that the first person avoids setbacks. It's that they return faster. They've learned that a break in the loop isn't the end of the loop. It's a pause. And the way you restart isn't by producing something brilliant. It's by producing something. Anything. A 60-second video just for yourself. A voice note to a friend. Even writing down what you would say if you were recording. The bar for re-entry can be as low as it needs to be. What matters is that you step back in.

Negative feedback is its own kind of break, and it deserves a specific kind of attention. Not all feedback carries the same weight. A comment from someone who understands your work and your audience is worth sitting with. A drive-by criticism from a stranger who watched ten seconds of one video is not. Learning to tell the difference is a skill in itself, and it protects the loop from being disrupted by noise that was never meant for you.

Comparison works differently. It doesn't arrive as a single blow. It accumulates. You watch someone who seems further ahead, and you don't feel crushed immediately. You just feel slightly less. Then you watch another, and the feeling deepens. The antidote isn't to stop watching other people's work. It's to notice when watching stops being inspiring and starts being corrosive, and to redirect your attention to your own path before the spiral takes hold.

None of these disruptions need to be permanent. The loop is resilient precisely because it isn't built on a single moment of confidence. It's built on a pattern of returning. Each time you come back after a break, you prove something to yourself that no unbroken streak could: that you can lose it and find it again. That the switch doesn't break. It just needs to be flipped again.

The Ripple Effect

As the loop strengthens, something unexpected happens. The confidence you've been building for the camera starts showing up in rooms that have nothing to do with content.

You notice it in a meeting where you speak up without rehearsing what you're going to say first. In a conversation where you hold your ground instead of softening your point. In the willingness to take on a visible role you would have declined a year ago. The presence you've been practising in front of a lens starts becoming the way you carry yourself everywhere.

This happens because the core shifts in this book were never really about cameras. Performance to presence. Approval-seeking to service. Perfectionism to progress. These are life shifts. The camera was just the place where you learned to make them.

One of my clients put it simply: "Learning to be myself on camera taught me how to be myself everywhere else. Once I stopped performing for the lens, I realised how much I'd been performing in the rest of my life too."

That's the real promise of the confidence switch. Not just better content. Not just a more comfortable relationship with recording. A deeper trust in your capacity to show up as yourself, in every context that asks you to.

And there's something else that happens, something you may never see directly. When you show up authentically, you give other people permission to do the same. Your willingness to be imperfect in public creates space for someone else to begin. Your consistency models what's possible. Your presence, however quiet, becomes an invitation.

You may not know whose first video was inspired by yours. You may not see the person who finally hit record because they watched you do it imperfectly and thought, *if they can, maybe I can too*. But those ripples are real. And they matter more than metrics ever will.

Reality Check: Confidence Isn't Static

MYTH #1: "Once I build confidence,
I'll never struggle again."

Even the most experienced creators have days when presence feels harder to find. Confidence isn't a destination you arrive at and stay. It's a practice that has strong days and weaker ones. The difference between someone who looks permanently confident and someone who doesn't isn't the absence of doubt. It's how quickly they return to their baseline after doubt shows up.

MYTH #2: "I need constant external
validation to maintain confidence."

Sustainable confidence comes from knowing your value regardless of the external response. The creators with the most durable confidence have clear internal markers for whether they're on the right track, markers that don't depend on likes, comments or conversion rates. Positive feedback is welcome when it arrives. But it's not the foundation. The foundation is the practice itself.

MYTH #3: "I need to completely
eliminate my inner critic."

The goal isn't silence. It's a different relationship. That critical voice often contains something useful when you approach it with curiosity rather than fear. The most confident creators haven't eliminated self-doubt. They've learned to hear it without being controlled by it, to extract what's valuable and let the rest pass.

MYTH #4: "More tools, techniques and training will make me more confident."

Confidence doesn't come from accumulating more knowledge or better equipment. It comes from consistent application of what you already know. The pursuit of more information is one of the most sophisticated forms of procrastination, because it feels productive while keeping you safely on the sidelines. You already have what you need. The loop is waiting for action, not preparation.

MYTH #5: "Confidence means getting comfortable."

Sustainable confidence isn't the absence of discomfort. It's an expanded capacity to act while experiencing it. Growth happens at the edges, not in the centre. The most confident creators haven't eliminated the butterflies. They've learned to work with them, recognising discomfort as a sign of expansion rather than a warning to retreat.

The Shift: Where It All Led

When I look back at where this started, it's hard to believe the distance.

The one-take method began as a way to solve a problem. I couldn't keep spending days trying to record a single video. Something had to change. So I stopped editing, stopped retaking, stopped trying to manufacture a version of myself that looked and sounded the way I thought a professional should. I just started showing up and sharing what I knew.

That single decision changed everything that followed. Not overnight, and not in ways I could have predicted. But the ability to create content without the weight of perfectionism meant I could create more of it. And creating more meant connecting with more people, more deeply, more often. The content wasn't polished. It was present. And that turned out to be what people actually responded to.

From there, the momentum built quietly. The courses and programmes I'd been stalling on for months came together in days. The live events I'd been too cautious to attempt became some of the most fulfilling work I've ever done. Take One Tech grew from a seed of an idea into something that genuinely helps people build businesses rooted in connection rather than performance.

But the part I didn't expect was how far beyond content the ripple would reach. Somewhere along the way, I realised I'd built something that gave me freedoms I hadn't consciously been chasing. The financial freedom to do work I believe in on my own terms. The time to be present with the people who matter. The ability to work from wherever I choose. And perhaps most importantly, the mental freedom of no longer being trapped in the cycle of perfectionism and performance that had quietly run so much of my earlier life.

It sounds bold to say that all of this traces back to being

more confident on camera. But it does. That was the seed. The willingness to show up imperfectly, to trust that presence was enough, to stop waiting for a version of myself that was never coming. Everything else grew from there.

The Japanese have a word for it: Ikigai. Your reason for being. The intersection of what you're good at, what you love, what the world needs and what sustains you. I didn't find mine through strategy or planning. I found it by pressing record and letting myself be seen.

Flip the Switch: Sustaining the Loop

These final exercises aren't about learning something new. They're about protecting what you've already built.

Exercise 1: Your Consistency Commitment

Choose a creation rhythm you can realistically sustain even during your busiest weeks. Not ideal-world frequency. Real-world frequency. Write it down as a specific commitment: what you'll create, when you'll create it and where it will go. The simpler and more specific this is, the more likely you are to keep it.

Exercise 2: The Progress Look-back

Gather three to five pieces of content you've created over time, ideally spanning several months or longer. Watch or read them in order. Don't judge them. Just notice the changes. Where has your presence grown? Where has your voice become more natural? What's different about how you show up now compared to when you started? This evidence is more persuasive than any motivational statement.

Exercise 3: The Return Plan

Write down what you'll do when the loop breaks, because it will. Keep it simple: one small action you'll take to step back in (a 60-second video, a voice note, even writing down what you'd say). One person you'll reach out to for support. One reminder of why you started. Put this somewhere you'll find it when you need it.

Exercise 4: The Honest Reflection

After your next piece of content, sit with three questions: What moments felt most present and connected? What pulled me out of presence and into performance? What would I like to try differently next time? This isn't a performance review. It's a way of paying attention to what the loop is teaching you.

Exercise 5: Make It Real

Record a short video, no more than two minutes, answering this question: What has changed for you since you started reading this book? Don't script it. Don't rehearse it. Just speak. This is your evidence that the switch is real, in your own voice, in your own words. Keep it. Come back to it on the days when you need reminding.

The power was never something you needed to find. It was something you needed to stop hiding from.

INTEGRATING PART FOUR

From Practice to Permanence

In these final chapters, we've explored how to make the confidence switch not just something you flip, but something that stays on.

• Authenticity is what your audience responds to most, and it asks nothing of you except to be yourself.

• The switch works in every format. Only the triggers change.

• Confidence sustains itself through a loop: show up, connect, return, repeat.

As you close this book, consider what's actually shifted for you. Not just in how you think about the camera, but in how you think about showing up. Where else in your life might you carry this same switch from performance to presence?

The confidence you've found here isn't limited to content. It's available in any moment you choose connection over performance.

THE JOURNEY AHEAD

So here we are.

Not at the end of something, but at the beginning of a different kind of practice. You didn't need to become someone else to get here. You just needed to see what was already true: that confidence was never something you lacked. It was something you'd been talked out of.

This book was my attempt to talk you back into it. Not with hype or motivation, but with the quiet, steady argument that you already have what it takes to show up, speak and be seen.

I hope that argument landed. But more than that, I hope you felt it. Not just understood it, but recognised it as something you already knew.

A Final Thought

I want to share something personal before we close.

My own journey with camera confidence wasn't linear. There were setbacks, moments of doubt, stretches where I questioned whether I was on the right path. Even now, years into creating content regularly, I still have days when the old stories try to reassert themselves. Days when I wonder if I've said enough, or said it well enough, or whether anyone is actually listening.

But here's what I know for certain. The decision to prioritise presence over perfection, to value connection over performance, to show up consistently even when it's uncomfortable, has been transformative. Not just for my content, but for my entire life. It's allowed me to reach people I never would have reached, to build a business I care about, to share ideas that matter to me. More importantly, it's freed me from the exhausting cycle of perfectionism and people-pleasing that kept me playing small for longer than I'd like to admit.

That freedom is available to you too. Not someday, when you've mastered some elusive set of skills. But now. The moment you decide to Flip the Switch.

If you ever find yourself slipping back into the old stories, about not being good enough or ready enough or polished enough, come back to this: you were never afraid of the camera. Just the story you told yourself about what would happen when you turned it on.

You know how to change that story now. So keep showing up. Keep speaking. Keep trusting that your voice matters.

It does.

The Journey Continues

If you'd like to revisit the Flip the Switch exercises, the free companion workbook is available at confidenceswitch.com.

If you want support, structure and a community of people who are doing this alongside you, I'd love to welcome you into the Digital Stage Academy. We go beyond confidence into creation, clarity, content strategy and building a business rooted in genuine connection. Because everything we've explored in this book, showing up, being seen, speaking to real people, isn't just how you create better content. It's how you grow something that lasts.

Whether you're just beginning or ready to take things

further, the Academy is here for you. You can find out more at: takeonetech.io/academy

Thank you for reading. Thank you for showing up.

Alec Johnson

Founder, Take One Tech

Creator, Digital Stage Academy

ABOUT THE AUTHOR

Alec Johnson is the founder of Take One Tech and the creator of the Digital Stage Academy, where he helps entrepreneurs, educators and change-makers show up confidently on camera and build businesses rooted in genuine connection.

After years of running live events around the world, from London to Dubai to Bangkok, Alec found himself stuck when it came to video. A perfectionist at heart, he struggled to translate his real-life presence into confident content in front of a lens. The turning point came when he adopted a one-take, live production workflow. Everything shifted, not just his content creation process, but his relationship with confidence itself.

Through his courses, coaching programmes and content, Alec has helped thousands of creators overcome their fear of being on camera and embrace video as a tool for connection, not performance.

He lives in Thailand with his wife and three children, where he records nearly everything in one take, practises what he preaches, and always reminds his students that confidence isn't something you find. It's something you remember.

Connect and Explore More

For additional resources and to continue the work you've started in this book, visit: confidenceswitch.com

You can also connect with Alec and the Take One Tech community here:

- Email: takeonetech.io/contact
- YouTube: youtube.com/c/TakeOneTech
- LinkedIn: linkedin.com/in/alec-w-johnson
- Facebook: facebook.com/TakeOneTech
- TikTok: tiktok.com/@TakeOneTech
- Instagram: instagram.com/takeonetech_